CHEESECAKES
AND
FLANS

CHEESECAKES
AND
FLANS

General Editor: Rhona Newman

LANGHAM PRESS

First published 1983 by Langham Press, Langham Park,
Catteshall Lane, Godalming, Surrey

In association with Octopus Books Limited,
59 Grosvenor Street,
London W1

© 1983 Octopus Books Limited

ISBN 0 86362 011 6

Produced by Mandarin Publishers Limited
22a Westlands Road, Quarry Bay, Hong Kong

Printed in Hong Kong

CONTENTS

NOTES
Standard spoon measurements are used in all recipes
1 tablespoon = one 15 ml spoon
1 teaspoon = one 5 ml spoon
All spoon measures are level

Fresh herbs are used unless otherwise stated. If
unobtainable, substitute a bouquet garni of the equivalent
dried herbs, or use dried herbs instead but halve the
quantities stated.
Ovens and grills (broilers) should be preheated to
specified temperature or heat setting.
For all recipes, quantities are given in metric, imperial and
American measures. Follow one set of measures only,
because they are not interchangeable.

MEAT AND FISH QUICHES AND FLANS

A meat or fish quiche served with salad or a hot vegetable makes a filling main course. Cut into smaller portions, these dishes can be served as starters too.

BEEF AND SPINACH FLAN (PIE)

METRIC/IMPERIAL	AMERICAN
Flan case	*Pie shell*
175 g/6 oz plain flour	1½ cups all-purpose flour
pinch of salt	pinch of salt
40 g/1½ oz margarine	3 tablespoons margarine
40 g/1½ oz lard	3 tablespoons shortening
50 g/2 oz cheese, grated	½ cup grated cheese
1–2 tablespoons water	1–2 tablespoons water
Filling	*Filling*
50 g/2 oz butter	¼ cup butter
1 onion, chopped	1 onion, chopped
175 g/6 oz minced beef	¾ cup ground beef
salt and pepper	salt and pepper
1 tablespoon plain flour	1 tablespoon all-purpose flour
1 × 225 g/8 oz packet frozen spinach	1 × ½ lb package frozen spinach
1 egg	1 egg
5 tablespoons single cream	5 tablespoons light cream
50 g/2 oz cheese, grated	½ cup grated cheese
Garnish	*Garnish*
1 tomato, sliced	tomato, sliced

Sift the flour and salt into a bowl and rub (cut) in the margarine and lard (shortening) until the mixture resembles fine breadcrumbs. Stir in the cheese and mix to a stiff dough with the water. Turn on to a floured surface and knead until smooth. Roll out and line a 20 cm/8 inch flan ring on a baking sheet. Line with greaseproof (parchment) paper and dried beans and 'bake blind' in a preheated moderately hot oven (190°C/375°F, Gas Mark 5) for 10 minutes. Remove the paper and beans and return to the oven for 5 minutes.

Melt 25 g/1 oz (2 tablespoons) of the butter in a pan and sauté the onion for 5 minutes. Add the beef and cook, mixing thoroughly, for 15 minutes. Stir in salt and pepper and the flour, then cook gently for 5 minutes, stirring well. Leave to cool.

Cook the spinach as directed on the packet. Melt the remaining butter in a pan and add the spinach. Heat gently, stirring, for 5 minutes. Add salt and pepper to taste. Layer the spinach and meat mixture in the flan case (pie shell).

Beat together the egg and cream, then stir in the cheese and salt and pepper to taste. Pour over the filling and return the flan (pie) to the oven for 20 to 30 minutes or until cooked and golden. Serve hot, garnished with tomato.

Serves 4 to 6

Beef and Spinach Flan; Chicken and Walnut Quiche

KIDNEY AND ONION QUICHE

METRIC/IMPERIAL	AMERICAN
Flan case	*Pie shell*
75 g/3 oz plain flour	¾ cup all-purpose flour
75 g/3 oz wholewheat flour	¾ cup wholewheat flour
pinch of salt	pinch of salt
½ teaspoon dried mixed herbs	½ teaspoon dried mixed herbs
75 g/3 oz margarine	⅓ cup margarine
1–2 tablespoons water	1–2 tablespoons water
Filling	*Filling*
25 g/1 oz butter	2 tablespoons butter
1 large onion, sliced	1 large onion, sliced
6 lambs' kidneys, cored and sliced	6 lambs' kidneys, cored and sliced
3 eggs	3 eggs
6 tablespoons single cream	6 tablespoons light cream
½ teaspoon dried mixed herbs	½ teaspoon dried mixed herbs
salt and pepper	salt and pepper

Mix the flours and salt in a bowl and stir in the herbs. Rub (cut) in the margarine until the mixture resembles fine breadcrumbs. Mix to a stiff dough with the water. Turn on to a floured surface and knead until smooth. Roll out and line a 20 cm/8 inch flan dish (pie pan).

To make the filling: melt the butter in a pan and sauté the onion for 5 minutes. Add the kidneys and cook for 5 to 10 minutes. Leave to cool then place in the flan case (pie shell).

Beat together the eggs and cream, then add the herbs and salt and pepper to taste. Pour over the kidneys and onions, then cook in a preheated moderately hot oven (190°C/375°F, Gas Mark 5) for 35 to 40 minutes or until firm and golden. Serve hot.
Serves 4 to 6

CHICKEN AND WALNUT QUICHE

METRIC/IMPERIAL	AMERICAN
Flan case	*Pie shell*
175 g/6 oz plain flour	1½ cups all-purpose flour
pinch of salt	pinch of salt
40 g/1½ oz margarine	3 tablespoons margarine
40 g/1½ oz lard	3 tablespoons shortening
1–2 tablespoons water	1–2 tablespoons water
Filling	*Filling*
175 g/6 oz cooked chicken, diced	¾ cup diced cooked chicken
50 g/2 oz walnuts, chopped	½ cup chopped walnuts
2 eggs	2 eggs
150 ml/¼ pint single cream	⅔ cup light cream
salt and pepper	salt and pepper
50 g/2 oz Parmesan cheese, grated	½ cup grated Parmesan cheese
Garnish	*Garnish*
walnut halves	walnut halves
parsley sprigs	parsley sprigs

Sift the flour and salt into a bowl and rub (cut) in the margarine and lard (shortening) until the mixture resembles fine breadcrumbs. Mix to a stiff dough with the water. Turn on to a floured surface and knead until smooth. Roll out and line a 20 cm/8 inch flan dish (pie pan).

Place the chicken and walnuts in the flan case (pie shell). Beat together the eggs, cream and salt and pepper to taste. Pour into the case (shell) and sprinkle with the cheese. Cook in a preheated moderately hot oven (190°C/375°F, Gas Mark 5) for 30 to 40 minutes or until firm and golden.

Serve hot or cold, garnished with walnuts and parsley.
Serves 4 to 6

SALAMI AND WATERCRESS QUICHE

METRIC/IMPERIAL	AMERICAN
Flan case	*Pie shell*
175 g/6 oz plain flour	1½ cups all-purpose flour
pinch of salt	pinch of salt
40 g/1½ oz margarine	3 tablespoons margarine
40 g/1½ oz lard	3 tablespoons shortening
1–2 tablespoons water	1–2 tablespoons water
Filling	*Filling*
25 g/1 oz butter	2 tablespoons butter
1 onion, sliced	1 onion, sliced
1 bunch of watercress, washed and chopped	1 bunch watercress, washed and chopped
75 g/3 oz salami, chopped	⅓ cup chopped salami
2 eggs	2 eggs
150 ml/¼ pint single cream	⅔ cup light cream
5 tablespoons milk	5 tablespoons milk
salt and pepper	salt and pepper
Garnish	*Garnish*
thinly sliced salami	thinly sliced salami
1 tomato, sliced	1 tomato, sliced

Sift the flour and salt into a bowl and rub (cut) in the margarine and lard (shortening) until the mixture resembles fine bread-crumbs. Mix to a stiff dough with the water. Turn on to a floured surface and knead until smooth. Roll out and line a 20 cm/8 inch flan ring on a baking sheet. Line with greaseproof (parchment) paper and dried beans and 'bake blind' in a preheated moderately hot oven (190°C/375°F, Gas Mark 5) for 15 minutes. Remove the paper and beans and continue to cook for 5 minutes. Leave to cool slightly.

Melt the butter in a pan and sauté the onion for 5 minutes. Add the watercress and cook for 3 minutes. Place in the flan case (pie shell) and top with the salami. Beat together the eggs, cream and milk. Add salt and pepper to taste, then pour over the salami and watercress. Return to the oven for 30 minutes or until firm and golden.

Remove the flan ring and place the quiche on a serving plate. Serve hot or cold, garnished with salami and tomato. Serves 4 to 6

Salami and Watercress Quiche

HAM AND TOMATO FLAN (PIE)

METRIC/IMPERIAL	AMERICAN
Base	*Base*
1 × 212 g/7½ oz packet frozen puff pastry, thawed	1 × ½ lb package frozen puff dough, thawed
Filling	*Filling*
175 g/6 oz cooked ham, sliced	¾ cup sliced cooked ham
450 g/1 lb tomatoes, skinned and sliced	2 cups peeled and sliced tomatoes
2 eggs	2 eggs
150 ml/¼ pint double cream	⅔ cup heavy cream
salt and pepper	salt and pepper
100 g/4 oz Cheddar cheese, sliced	¼ lb sliced Cheddar cheese
black olives, stoned	ripe olives, pitted
Garnish	*Garnish*
parsley sprigs	parsley sprigs

Roll out the pastry and line a 28 × 18 cm (11 × 7 inches) Swiss roll tin (jelly roll pan).

Cover the base with the ham and arrange the tomatoes on top. Beat together the eggs, cream, and salt and pepper to taste, then pour over the tomatoes.

Arrange the cheese slices on top with the olives. Cook in a preheated hot oven (220°C/425°F, Gas Mark 7) for 35 to 40 minutes or until cooked and golden. Serve hot, garnished with parsley. Serves 6 to 8

SPICED MEAT FLAN (PIE)

METRIC/IMPERIAL	AMERICAN
Filling	*Filling*
100 g/4 oz cooked chicken	$\frac{1}{2}$ cup cooked chicken
100 g/4 oz cooked ham	$\frac{1}{2}$ cup cooked ham
15 g/$\frac{1}{2}$ oz margarine	1 tablespoon margarine
1 onion, finely chopped	1 onion, minced
1 clove garlic, crushed	1 clove garlic, crushed
$\frac{1}{2}$ teaspoon ground turmeric	$\frac{1}{2}$ teaspoon ground turmeric
$\frac{1}{2}$ teaspoon ground ginger	$\frac{1}{2}$ teaspoon ground ginger
$\frac{1}{2}$ teaspoon ground cumin	$\frac{1}{2}$ teaspoon ground cumin
1 teaspoon made mustard	1 teaspoon made mustard
150 ml/$\frac{1}{4}$ pint plain yogurt	$\frac{2}{3}$ cup plain yogurt
salt and pepper	salt and pepper
Flan case	*Pie shell*
175 g/6 oz plain flour	1$\frac{1}{2}$ cups all-purpose flour
pinch of salt	pinch of salt
1 teaspoon curry powder	1 teaspoon curry powder
75 g/3 oz margarine	$\frac{1}{3}$ cup margarine
1–2 tablespoons water	1–2 tablespoons water
Garnish	*Garnish*
2 small tomatoes, sliced	2 small tomatoes, sliced
parsley	parsley

Put the chicken and ham through a mincer (grinder). Melt the margarine in a pan and sauté the onion and garlic for 5 minutes. Add the turmeric, ginger and cumin and cook for a further 5 minutes. Stir in the meat and cook for 1 minute. Remove from the heat and stir in the mustard, yogurt and salt and pepper to taste. Cover and place in the refrigerator for a few hours to enable the flavour to penetrate into the meat.

Sift the flour, salt and curry powder into a bowl and rub (cut) in the margarine until the mixture resembles fine bread-crumbs. Mix to a stiff dough with the water. Turn on to a floured surface and knead until smooth. Roll out and line a 20 cm/8 inch flan ring on a baking sheet. Line with greaseproof (parchment) paper and dried beans and 'bake blind' in a preheated moderately hot oven (190°C/375°F, Gas Mark 5) for 15 minutes. Remove the paper and beans and return to the oven for 5 minutes. Leave to cool slightly, then remove the ring and place the flan case (pie shell) on a serving plate.

Spoon the filling into the flan (pie) and garnish with tomato and parsley.
Serves 4 to 6

SPANISH FLAN (PIE)

METRIC/IMPERIAL	AMERICAN
Flan case	*Pie shell*
175 g/6 oz plain flour	1$\frac{1}{2}$ cups all-purpose flour
pinch of salt	pinch of salt
75 g/3 oz margarine	$\frac{1}{3}$ cup margarine
1–2 tablespoons water	1–2 tablespoons water
Filling	*Filling*
2 tablespoons oil	2 tablespoons oil
2 onions, chopped	2 onions, chopped
1 clove garlic, crushed	1 clove garlic, crushed
75 g/3 oz garlic sausage, chopped	$\frac{1}{3}$ cup chopped garlic sausage
6 stuffed green olives, sliced	6 stuffed green olives, sliced
2 eggs	2 eggs
150 ml/$\frac{1}{4}$ pint single cream	$\frac{2}{3}$ cup light cream
$\frac{1}{2}$ teaspoon dried basil	$\frac{1}{2}$ teaspoon dried basil
salt and pepper	salt and pepper

Sift the flour and salt into a bowl and rub (cut) in the margarine until the mixture resembles fine breadcrumbs. Mix to a stiff dough with the water. Turn on to a floured surface and knead until smooth. Roll out and line a 20 cm/8 inch flan dish (pie pan).

Heat the oil in a pan and sauté the onions and garlic for 5 minutes. Place in the flan case (pie shell) with the garlic sausage and olives. Beat together the eggs, cream, basil and salt and pepper to taste. Pour over the filling and cook in a preheated moderately hot oven (190°C/375°F, Gas Mark 5) for 35 to 40 minutes or until firm and golden. Serve hot or cold.
Serves 4 to 6

SAUSAGE AND BACON FLAN (PIE)

METRIC/IMPERIAL	AMERICAN
Flan case	*Pie shell*
175 g/6 oz plain flour	1½ cups all-purpose flour
pinch of salt	pinch of salt
½ teaspoon dried mixed herbs	½ teaspoon dried mixed herbs
75 g/3 oz margarine	⅓ cup margarine
1–2 tablespoons water	1–2 tablespoons water
Filling	*Filling*
3 pork sausages, cooked	3 pork sausage links, cooked
25 g/1 oz margarine	2 tablespoons margarine
1 small onion, chopped	1 small onion, chopped
50 g/2 oz streaky bacon, chopped	3 fatty bacon slices, chopped
25 g/1 oz plain flour	¼ cup all-purpose flour
200 ml/⅓ pint milk	⅞ cup milk
½ teaspoon dried sage	½ teaspoon dried sage
salt and pepper	salt and pepper
Garnish	*Garnish*
watercress	watercress

Sift the flour and salt into a bowl and stir in the herbs. Rub (cut) in the margarine until the mixture resembles fine breadcrumbs. Mix to a stiff dough with the water. Turn on to a floured surface and knead until smooth. Roll out and line a 20 cm/8 inch flan dish (pie pan). Line with greaseproof (parchment) paper and dried beans and 'bake blind' in a preheated moderately hot oven (190°C/375°F, Gas Mark 5) for 10 minutes. Remove the paper and beans and continue to cook for 5 minutes.

Slice the sausages and place in the flan case (pie shell). Melt the margarine in a pan and sauté the onion until soft, then add the bacon and cook for 5 minutes. Stir in the flour and cook for 1 minute. Remove from the heat and gradually blend in the milk. Cook the sauce, stirring, until it thickens. Stir in the sage and salt and pepper to taste. Spoon over the sausages and return to the oven for 20 minutes. Serve hot, garnished with watercress.

Serves 4 to 6

ITALIAN PIZZA FLAN (PIE)

METRIC/IMPERIAL	AMERICAN
Base	*Base*
175 g/6 oz plain flour	1½ cups all-purpose flour
pinch of salt	pinch of salt
75 g/3 oz margarine	⅓ cup margarine
½ teaspoon dried mixed herbs	½ teaspoon dried mixed herbs
1–2 tablespoons water	1–2 tablespoons water
Filling	*Filling*
2 tablespoons oil	2 tablespoons oil
450 g/1 lb onions, sliced	4 cups sliced onion
2 cloves garlic, crushed	2 cloves garlic, crushed
1 × 400 g/14 oz can tomatoes	1 × 1 lb can tomatoes
1 teaspoon dried oregano	1 teaspoon dried oregano
salt and pepper	salt and pepper
75 g/3 oz Mozzarella cheese, grated	¾ cup grated Mozzarella cheese
2 × 50 g/2 oz cans anchovy fillets, drained	2 × 2 oz cans anchovy fillets, drained
black olives	ripe olives
oil	oil

Sift the flour and salt into a bowl and rub (cut) in the margarine until the mixture resembles fine breadcrumbs. Stir in the herbs and mix to a stiff dough with the water. Turn on to a floured surface and knead until smooth. Roll out to a rectangle 30 × 18 cm (12 × 7 inches) and place on a baking sheet. Turn up the edges to make a rim.

Heat the oil in a pan and sauté the onions and garlic for 10 minutes. Add the tomatoes with their juice, oregano and salt and pepper to taste. Bring to the boil, then simmer until the onions are cooked and the liquid has reduced by one-third.

Spread the mixture over the pastry case (pie shell) and sprinkle with the cheese.

Cut the anchovies in half lengthwise and arrange in a lattice pattern over the flan (pie). Cut the olives in half and remove the stones (seeds). Arrange in the spaces between the anchovies. Brush the surface with oil and cook in a preheated moderately hot oven (200°C/400°F, Gas Mark 6) for 20 to 25 minutes. Serve hot or cold.

Serves 4 to 6

TUNA AND CORN FLAN (PIE)

METRIC/IMPERIAL	AMERICAN
Flan case	*Pie shell*
175 g/6 oz plain flour	1½ cups all-purpose flour
pinch of salt	pinch of salt
40 g/1½ oz margarine	3 tablespoons margarine
40 g/1½ oz lard	3 tablespoons shortening
50 g/2 oz Cheddar cheese, grated	½ cup grated cheese
1–2 tablespoons water	1–2 tablespoons water
Filling	*Filling*
15 g/½ oz butter	1 tablespoon butter
1 onion, finely chopped	1 onion, finely chopped
1 × 200 g/7 oz can tuna, drained	1 × 7 oz can tuna, drained
1 × 225 g/8 oz can tomatoes, drained	1 × ½ lb can tomatoes, drained
6 tablespoons sweetcorn	6 tablespoons whole kernel corn
2 eggs	2 eggs
150 ml/¼ pint single cream	⅔ cup light cream
salt and pepper	salt and pepper
Garnish	*Garnish*
tomato segments	tomato segments
watercress	watercress

Sift the flour and salt into a bowl and rub (cut) in the margarine and lard (shortening) until the mixture resembles fine bread-crumbs. Stir in the cheese, then mix to a stiff dough with the water. Turn on to a floured surface and knead until smooth. Roll out and line a 20 cm/8 inch flan dish (pie pan).

Melt the butter in a pan and fry the onion until soft, then place in the flan case (pie shell). Flake the tuna and place in the flan (shell) with the tomatoes and corn. Beat the eggs and cream together and add salt and pepper to taste. Pour over the other ingredients in the flan (shell). Cook in a preheated moderately hot oven (200°C/400°F, Gas Mark 6) for 25 to 35 minutes or until firm and golden. Serve hot or cold, garnished with tomato and watercress.

Serves 4 to 6

Sausage and Bacon Flan (Pie); Tuna and Corn Flan (Pie); Pork and Bean Flan (Pie)

PORK AND BEAN FLAN (PIE)

METRIC/IMPERIAL	AMERICAN
Flan case	*Pie shell*
175 g/6 oz plain flour	1½ cups all-purpose flour
pinch of salt	pinch of salt
40 g/1½ oz margarine	3 tablespoons margarine
40 g/1½ oz lard	3 tablespoons shortening
1–2 tablespoons water	1–2 tablespoons water
Filling	*Filling*
40 g/1½ oz butter	3 tablespoons butter
25 g/1 oz plain flour	¼ cup all-purpose flour
150 ml/¼ pint milk	⅔ cup milk
150 ml/¼ pint single cream	⅔ cup light cream
100 g/4 oz cooked green beans	½ cup cooked green beans
100 g/4 oz cooked broad beans	1 cup cooked lima beans
100 g/4 oz cooked pork, diced	½ cup diced cooked pork
1 tablespoon chopped chives	1 tablespoon chopped chives
salt and pepper	salt and pepper
Garnish	*Garnish*
parsley sprigs	parsley sprigs

Sift the flour and salt into a bowl and rub (cut) in the margarine and lard (shortening) until the mixture resembles fine bread-crumbs. Mix to a stiff dough with the water. Turn on to a floured surface and knead until smooth. Roll out and line a 20 cm/8 inch flan dish (pie pan). Line with greaseproof (parchment) paper and dried beans and 'bake blind' in a preheated moderately hot oven (190°C/375°F, Gas Mark 5) for 15 minutes. Remove the paper and beans and return to the oven for 5 to 10 minutes.

Melt the butter in a pan and stir in the flour, then cook for 1 minute. Remove from the heat and gradually blend in the milk and cream. Cook the sauce, stirring, until it thickens. Stir in the green beans, broad (lima) beans, pork, chives and salt and pepper to taste. Heat through and spoon into the cooked flan case (pie shell). Serve immediately, garnished with parsley.

Serves 4 to 6

CURRIED FISH QUICHE

METRIC/IMPERIAL	AMERICAN
Flan case	*Pie shell*
175 g/6 oz plain flour	1½ cups all-purpose flour
pinch of salt	pinch of salt
1 teaspoon curry powder	1 teaspoon curry powder
40 g/1½ oz margarine	3 tablespoons margarine
40 g/1½ oz lard	3 tablespoons shortening
1–2 tablespoons water	1–2 tablespoons water
Filling	*Filling*
50 g/2 oz butter	¼ cup butter
1 onion, chopped	1 onion, chopped
2 teaspoons curry powder	2 teaspoons curry powder
2 eggs, beaten	2 eggs, beaten
150 ml/¼ pint milk	⅔ cup milk
salt	salt
100 g/4 oz peeled prawns	⅔ cup shelled shrimp
225 g/8 oz white fish, diced	½ lb diced white fish
Garnish	*Garnish*
parsley sprigs	parsley sprigs
unpeeled prawns	unshelled shrimp

Sift the flour, salt and curry powder into a bowl and rub (cut) in the margarine and lard (shortening) until the mixture resembles fine breadcrumbs. Mix to a stiff dough with the water. Turn on to a floured surface and knead until smooth. Roll out and line a 20 cm/8 inch flan dish (pie pan).

Melt the butter in a pan and sauté the onion for 5 minutes. Add the curry powder and cook for 2 minutes. Leave to cool.

Mix together the eggs and milk, then add the curry mixture and salt to taste. Arrange the prawns (shrimp) and fish in the flan case (pie shell) and pour over the curry mixture. Cook in a preheated moderately hot oven (190°C/375°F, Gas Mark 5) for 30 to 40 minutes or until firm. Serve hot, garnished with parsley and unpeeled prawns (shrimp).
Serves 4 to 6

CREAMY CRAB FLAN (PIE)

METRIC/IMPERIAL	AMERICAN
Base	*Base*
175 g/6 oz wholewheat flour	1½ cups wholewheat flour
pinch of salt	pinch of salt
75 g/3 oz butter	⅓ cup butter
2 tablespoons water	2 tablespoons water
Filling	*Filling*
225 g/8 oz crab meat	½ lb crab meat
2 eggs	2 eggs
300 ml/½ pint double cream	1¼ cups heavy cream
1 tablespoon chopped parsley	1 tablespoon chopped parsley
salt and pepper	salt and pepper
Garnish	*Garnish*
1 green pepper, cored, seeded and cut into rings	1 green pepper, seeded and sliced into rings

Place the flour and salt in a bowl and rub (cut) in the butter until the mixture resembles fine breadcrumbs. Mix to a stiff dough with the water. Turn on to a floured surface and knead until smooth. Roll out and line a 20 cm/8 inch flan (pie) ring on a baking sheet. Line with greaseproof (parchment) paper and dried beans and 'bake blind' in a preheated moderately hot oven (190°C/375°F, Gas Mark 5) for 10 minutes. Remove the paper and beans and return to the oven for 5 minutes.

Break up the crab meat with a fork and place in the pastry case (pie shell). Beat together the eggs, cream, parsley and salt and pepper to taste. Pour over the crab and cook in a moderately hot oven (190°C/375°F, Gas Mark 5) for 30 to 40 minutes until firm.

Remove the flan (pie) ring and place the flan (pie) on a serving plate. Serve hot, garnished with green pepper rings.
Serves 4 to 6

COD AND COURGETTE (ZUCCHINI) FLAN (PIE)

METRIC/IMPERIAL	AMERICAN
Flan case	*Pie shell*
75 g/3 oz plain flour	¾ cup all-purpose flour
75 g/3 oz wholewheat flour	¾ cup wholewheat flour
pinch of salt	pinch of salt
40 g/1½ oz margarine	3 tablespoons margarine
40 g/1½ oz lard	3 tablespoons shortening
50 g/2 oz cheese, grated	½ cup grated cheese
1–2 tablespoons water	1–2 tablespoons water
Filling	*Filling*
25 g/1 oz butter	2 tablespoons butter
225 g/8 oz courgettes, sliced	1¾ cups sliced zucchini
225 g/8 oz cod	½ lb cod
300 ml/½ pint milk	1¼ cups milk
50 g/2 oz margarine	¼ cup margarine
50 g/2 oz plain flour	½ cup plain flour
50 g/2 oz mature Cheddar cheese, grated	½ cup grated sharp Cheddar cheese
salt and pepper	salt and pepper

Mix the flours and salt in a bowl and rub (cut) in the margarine and lard (shortening) until the mixture resembles fine breadcrumbs. Stir in the cheese and mix to a stiff dough with the water. Turn on to a floured surface and knead until smooth. Roll out and line a 20 cm/8 inch flan dish (pie pan). Line with greaseproof (parchment) paper and dried beans and 'bake blind' in a preheated moderately hot oven (190°C/375°F, Gas Mark 5) for 10 minutes. Remove the paper and beans and return to the oven for 5 minutes.

Melt the butter in a pan and sauté the courgettes (zucchini) for 5 minutes. Place the cod and milk in a pan and poach for 10 minutes. Drain and reserve the liquid, then flake the fish, removing any skin and bones.

In another pan, melt the margarine, then stir in the flour and cook for 1 minute. Remove from the heat and gradually stir in the reserved milk. Cook the sauce, stirring, until it thickens. Stir in the cheese and add salt and pepper to taste. Add the courgettes (zucchini) and cod, then spoon into the pastry case (pie shell). Cook in a moderately hot oven (190°C/375°F, Gas Mark 5) for 15 to 20 minutes or until golden. Serve hot.
Serves 4 to 6

Curried Fish Quiche; Cod and Courgette (Zucchini) Flan (Pie); Creamy Crab Flan (Pie)

COTTAGE KIPPER QUICHE

METRIC/IMPERIAL	AMERICAN
Flan case	*Pie shell*
75 g/3 oz plain flour	¾ cup all-purpose flour
75 g/3 oz wholewheat flour	¾ cup wholewheat flour
pinch of salt	pinch of salt
40 g/1½ oz margarine	3 tablespoons margarine
40 g/1½ oz lard	3 tablespoons shortening
2 tablespoons water	2 tablespoons water
Filling	*Filling*
225 g/8 oz kipper fillets	½ lb kipper fillets
300 ml/½ pint water	1¼ cups water
225 g/8 oz cottage cheese	1 cup cottage cheese
juice of 1 lemon	juice of 1 lemon
½ green pepper, cored, seeded and chopped	½ green pepper, seeded and chopped
1 tablespoon chopped parsley	1 tablespoon chopped parsley
2 eggs, beaten	2 eggs, beaten
salt and pepper	salt and pepper
Garnish	*Garnish*
½ lemon, sliced	½ lemon, sliced
parsley sprigs	parsley sprigs

Mix the flours and salt into a bowl and rub (cut) in the margarine and lard (shortening) until the mixture resembles fine breadcrumbs. Mix to a stiff dough with the water. Turn on to a floured surface and knead until smooth. Roll out and line a 20 cm/8 inch flan dish (pie pan).

Place the kipper fillets in a pan and cover with the water. Bring to the boil, cover and simmer for 5 to 10 minutes or until cooked. Drain, remove any skin and bones, then flake the fish. Combine with the cottage cheese, lemon juice, green pepper, parsley and eggs. Mix well and add salt and pepper to taste. Pour into the pastry case (pie shell) and cook in a preheated moderately hot oven (190°C/375°F, Gas Mark 5) for 35 to 45 minutes or until firm and golden.

Serve the quiche hot, garnished with twisted lemon slices and parsley.
Serves 4 to 6

MACKEREL FLAN (PIE)

METRIC/IMPERIAL	AMERICAN
Flan case	*Pie shell*
175 g/6 oz plain flour	1½ cups all-purpose flour
pinch of salt	pinch of salt
40 g/1½ oz margarine	3 tablespoons margarine
40 g/1½ oz lard	3 tablespoons shortening
1–2 tablespoons water	1–2 tablespoons water
Filling	*Filling*
1 × 200 g/7 oz can mackerel fillets, drained	1 × 7 oz can mackerel fillets, drained
100 g/4 oz cooked rice	1 cup cooked rice
2 hard-boiled eggs, chopped	2 hard-cooked eggs, chopped
50 g/2 oz cucumber, diced	½ cup diced cucumber
2 tablespoons mayonnaise	2 tablespoons mayonnaise
1 teaspoon lemon juice	1 teaspoon lemon juice
2 teaspoons chopped chives	2 teaspoons chopped chives
2 teaspoons chopped parsley	2 teaspoons chopped parsley
salt and pepper	salt and pepper
Garnish	*Garnish*
thinly sliced cucumber	thinly sliced cucumber
parsley sprigs	parsley sprigs

Sift the flour and salt into a bowl and rub (cut) in the fats until the mixture resembles fine crumbs. Mix to a dough with water and knead until smooth. Roll out and line a 20 cm/8 inch flan (pie) ring on a baking sheet. Line with greaseproof (parchment) paper and dried beans and bake in a preheated moderate oven (190°C/375°F, Gas Mark 5) for 15 minutes. Remove the paper and beans and return to the oven for about 5 minutes. Cool, remove the ring and place the pastry case on a plate.

Flake the mackerel in a bowl. Stir in the remaining filling ingredients and season to taste. Spoon into the pastry case and garnish with cucumber and parsley. Serve lightly chilled.
Serves 4 to 6

Mackerel Flan (Pie); Seafood Quiche

SEAFOOD QUICHE

METRIC/IMPERIAL

Flan case
275 g/10 oz plain flour
pinch of salt
150 g/5 oz butter
1 egg, beaten
Filling
2 teaspoons oil
1 onion, chopped
225 g/8 oz tomatoes, skinned
  and chopped
1 × 227 g/8 oz can salmon
120 ml/4 fl oz milk
  (approximately)
1 × 80 g/3¼ oz can crab meat,
  drained
175 g/6 oz peeled prawns
3 eggs
100 g/4 oz Cheddar cheese,
  grated
salt and pepper
Garnish
lemon slices
whole unpeeled prawns

AMERICAN

Pie shell
2½ cups all-purpose flour
pinch of salt
½ cup plus 2 tablespoons
  butter
1 egg, beaten
Filling
2 teaspoons oil
1 onion, chopped
1 cup chopped peeled
  tomatoes
1 × ½ lb can salmon
½ cup milk (approximately)
1 × 3¼ oz can crabmeat,
  drained
1 cup shelled shrimp
3 eggs
1 cup grated Cheddar
  cheese
salt and pepper
Garnish
lemon slices
whole shrimp

Sift the flour and salt into a bowl and rub (cut) in the butter until the mixture resembles fine breadcrumbs. Mix to a stiff dough with the egg, adding a little water if necessary. Turn on to a floured surface and knead until smooth. Chill the dough for 30 minutes, then roll out and line a 25 cm/10 inch flan dish (pie pan). Line with greaseproof (parchment) paper and dried beans and 'bake blind' in a preheated moderately hot oven (190°C/375°F, Gas Mark 5), for 15 minutes. Remove the paper and beans and return to the oven for 5 minutes.

Heat the oil in a pan and sauté the onion for 5 minutes. Add the tomatoes and cook for 3 minutes.

Drain the salmon and reserve the liquid. Make up to 150 ml/¼ pint (⅔ cup) with the milk. Remove any skin and bones from the salmon and flake with the crab. Place in the flan case (pie shell) with the prawns (shrimp) and tomato mixture.

Beat together the eggs and milk mixture, then stir in the cheese and add salt and pepper to taste. Pour over the fish and cook in a preheated moderately hot oven (190°C/375°F, Gas Mark 5) for 30 to 35 minutes or until set and golden brown.

Serve hot or cold, garnished with lemon and prawns (shrimp).
Serves 10

INDIVIDUAL HADDOCK AND EGG QUICHES

METRIC/IMPERIAL	AMERICAN
Flan cases	*Pie shells*
175 g/6 oz plain flour	1½ cups all-purpose flour
pinch of salt	pinch of salt
75 g/3 oz margarine	⅓ cup margarine
50 g/2 oz Cheddar cheese, grated	½ cup grated Cheddar cheese
2 tablespoons water	2 tablespoons water
Filling	*Filling*
225 g/8 oz smoked haddock, cooked and flaked	½ lb finnan haddie, cooked and flaked
2 hard-boiled eggs, chopped	2 hard-cooked eggs, chopped
grated rind of ½ lemon	grated rind of ½ lemon
1 tablespoon chopped parsley	1 tablespoon chopped parsley
1 teaspoon made mustard	1 teaspoon prepared mustard
2 eggs, beaten	2 eggs, beaten
150 ml/¼ pint double cream	⅔ cup heavy cream
freshly ground black pepper	freshly ground black pepper
Garnish	*Garnish*
tomato slices	tomato slices
parsley	parsley

Sift the flour and salt into a bowl and rub (cut) in the margarine until the mixture resembles fine breadcrumbs. Stir in the cheese and mix to a stiff dough with the water. Turn on to a floured surface and knead until smooth. Roll out and line six 7.5 cm/3 inch flan cases (pie pans); stand on a baking sheet. Line with foil and 'bake blind' in a preheated moderately hot oven (190°C/375°F, Gas Mark 5) for 10 minutes.

Mix together the fish, eggs, lemon rind, parsley, mustard, beaten eggs, cream and pepper. Spoon into the flan cases (pie shells) and cook in a moderately hot oven (190°C/375°F, Gas Mark 5) for 25 minutes or until set and golden. Serve hot or cold, garnished with tomato and parsley.
Serves 6

SALMON AND CHEESE QUICHE

METRIC/IMPERIAL	AMERICAN
Flan case	*Pie shell*
100 g/4 oz plain flour	1 cup all-purpose flour
pinch of salt	pinch of salt
25 g/1 oz margarine	2 tablespoons margarine
25 g/1 oz lard	2 tablespoons shortening
1 tablespoon water	1 tablespoon water
Filling	*Filling*
15 g/½ oz butter	1 tablespoon butter
15 g/½ oz plain flour	2 tablespoons all-purpose flour
150 ml/¼ pint milk	⅔ cup milk
salt and pepper	salt and pepper
1 × 200 g/7 oz can salmon	1 × 7 oz can salmon
75 g/3 oz Cheddar cheese, grated	¾ cup grated Cheddar cheese
1 tablespoon grated Parmesan cheese	1 tablespoon grated Parmesan cheese
Garnish	*Garnish*
parsley sprigs	parsley sprigs
lemon twists	lemon twists

Sift the flour and salt into a bowl and rub (cut) in the margarine and lard (shortening) until the mixture resembles fine breadcrumbs. Mix to a stiff dough with the water. Turn on to a floured surface and knead until smooth. Roll out and line an 18 cm/7 inch flan dish (pie pan). Line with greaseproof (parchment) paper and dried beans and 'bake blind' in a preheated moderately hot oven (190°C/375°F, Gas Mark 5) for 10 to 15 minutes. Remove the paper and beans and return to the oven for 5 minutes.

Melt the butter in a pan, add the flour and cook for 1 minute. Remove from the heat and gradually blend in the milk. Cook the sauce, stirring, until it thickens. Add salt and pepper to taste.

Drain the salmon and add the liquid to the sauce. Flake the fish and add to the sauce with 50 g/2 oz of the cheese. Mix well and spoon into the pastry case (pie shell). Mix the remaining Cheddar cheese with the Parmesan and sprinkle over the top. Place under a preheated moderate grill (broiler) for 5 minutes to brown.

Serve hot or cold, garnished with parsley and lemon twists.
Serves 4 to 6

SMOKED SALMON QUICHE

METRIC/IMPERIAL	AMERICAN
Base	*Base*
175 g/6 oz plain flour	1½ cups all-purpose flour
pinch of salt	pinch of salt
75 g/3 oz margarine	⅓ cup margarine
1½ tablespoons cold water	1½ tablespoons cold water
Filling	*Filling*
100 g/4 oz smoked salmon, thinly sliced	¼ lb smoked salmon, thinly sliced
2 eggs	2 eggs
150 ml/¼ pint single cream	⅔ cup light cream
grated rind of ½ lemon	grated rind of ½ lemon
salt and pepper	salt and pepper
Garnish	*Garnish*
50 g/2 oz smoked salmon, thinly sliced and rolled	2 oz smoked salmon, thinly sliced and rolled
watercress	watercress

Sift the flour and salt into a bowl and rub (cut) in the margarine until the mixture resembles fine breadcrumbs. Mix to a stiff dough with the water. Turn on to a floured surface and knead until smooth. Roll out and line a 23 cm/9 inch long oval china flan dish (pie pan). Line with greaseproof (parchment) paper and dried beans and 'bake blind' in a preheated moderately hot oven (190°C/375°F, Gas Mark 5) for 10 minutes. Remove the paper and beans and return to the oven for 5 minutes.

Arrange the smoked salmon in the flan case (pie shell). Beat together the eggs and cream, then add the lemon rind and salt and pepper to taste. Pour over the salmon and cook in a preheated moderate oven (180°C/350°F, Gas Mark 4) for 30 minutes or until firm and golden.

Serve the quiche 1 hour after removing from the oven. Garnish with salmon rolls and watercress.
Serves 4 to 6

Smoked Salmon Quiche

VEGETABLE QUICHES AND FLANS

Vegetables, on their own or enhanced with nuts or interesting cheeses, make tasty and unusual fillings for quiches and flans. Serve these for a vegetarian meal, or with other kinds of quiche, for a buffet or party.

BROCCOLI AND ALMOND FLAN (PIE)

METRIC/IMPERIAL	AMERICAN
225 g/8 oz broccoli	$\frac{1}{2}$ lb broccoli
shortcrust pastry, made with 175 g/6 oz flour (page 94)	pie pastry made with $1\frac{1}{2}$ cups flour (page 94)
salt and pepper	salt and pepper
100 g/4 oz Edam cheese, grated	1 cup grated Edam cheese
2 eggs	2 eggs
150 ml/$\frac{1}{4}$ pint milk	$\frac{2}{3}$ cup milk
1 small clove garlic, crushed	1 small clove garlic, crushed
3 tablespoons flaked almonds	3 tablespoons flaked almonds

Cut the broccoli florets from the stalks. Peel and dice the stalks and break the florets into even pieces. Cook the broccoli in boiling salted water for 4 to 5 minutes until just tender. Drain well and leave to cool.

Roll out the pastry and line a 20 cm/8 inch flan tin (pie pan). Line with greaseproof (parchment) paper and dried beans and 'bake blind' in a preheated moderately hot oven (200°C/400°F, Gas Mark 6) for 15 minutes. Remove the paper and beans.

Sprinkle half the cheese over bottom of flan case (pie shell). Arrange the broccoli florets in circle around the outside edge of the flan (pie) and the diced pieces in the centre. Beat together the eggs, milk, garlic, salt and pepper to taste and remaining cheese and pour into the flan (pie). Sprinkle almonds on top and cook in a moderately hot oven (200°C/400°F, Gas Mark 6) for a further 25 minutes.
Serves 4 to 6

18

BLUE STILTON FLAN (PIE)

METRIC/IMPERIAL	AMERICAN
Flan case	*Pie shell*
225 g/8 oz plain flour	2 cups all-purpose flour
pinch of salt	pinch of salt
150 g/5 oz butter	$\frac{1}{2}$ cup plus 2 tablespoons
1 egg, beaten	butter
Filling	1 egg, beaten
knob of butter	*Filling*
1 large onion, finely	pat of butter
chopped	1 large onion, chopped
175 g/6 oz Blue Stilton,	1 cup crumbled Blue Stilton
crumbled	$1\frac{1}{4}$ cups heavy cream
300 ml/$\frac{1}{2}$ pint double cream	2 eggs
2 eggs	1 egg yolk
1 egg yolk	pepper
pepper	grated nutmeg
grated nutmeg	

Sift together the flour and salt and rub (cut) in the butter. Add the egg and work to a soft dough. Roll out and line a 25 cm/10 inch flan tin (pie pan). Line with greaseproof (parchment) paper and dried beans and 'bake blind' in a preheated moderately hot oven (200°C/400°F, Gas Mark 6) for 15 minutes. Remove the paper and beans.

Melt the butter in a pan and sauté the onion. Spread over the flan case (pie shell). Sprinkle the cheese on top. Beat together the cream, eggs, egg yolk with pepper and nutmeg to taste. Pour over the onion and cheese and cook in a moderately hot oven (190°C/375°F, Gas Mark 5) for 30 to 35 minutes until the filling is just firm.
Serves 6 to 8

WHOLEMEAL ASPARAGUS BOATS

Broccoli and Almond Flan (Pie); Wholemeal Asparagus Boats

METRIC/IMPERIAL	AMERICAN
Pastry	*Pie dough*
150 g/5 oz wholemeal flour	$1\frac{1}{4}$ cups wholewheat flour
$\frac{1}{4}$ teaspoon baking powder	$\frac{1}{4}$ teaspoon baking powder
pinch of salt	pinch of salt
75 g/3 oz butter	6 tablespoons butter
about 2 tablespoons water	about 2 tablespoons water
Filling	*Filling*
2 eggs	2 eggs
6 tablespoons single cream	6 tablespoons light cream
salt and pepper	salt and pepper
1 × 340 g/12 oz can	1 × 12 oz can asparagus
asparagus spears, drained	spears, drained
50 g/2 oz Gruyère cheese,	$\frac{1}{2}$ cup grated Gruyère cheese
grated	*Garnish*
Garnish	parsley sprigs
parsley sprigs	

Mix together the flour, baking powder and salt in a bowl. Rub (cut) in the butter until the mixture resembles fine breadcrumbs. Add sufficient water to make a soft dough. Roll out on a lightly floured surface and line six 15 cm/6 inch long boat-shaped moulds.

Beat together the eggs, cream and salt and pepper to taste. Divide the asparagus between the 'boats', pour the egg mixture carefully on top and sprinkle over the cheese. Cook in a preheated moderately hot oven (200°C/400°F, Gas Mark 6) for about 20 minutes until golden. Garnish with parsley.
Makes 6

EGG AND ARTICHOKE TARTLETS

METRIC/IMPERIAL	AMERICAN
Flan case	*Pie shell*
175 g/6 oz plain flour	1½ cups all-purpose flour
pinch of salt	pinch of salt
pinch of paprika pepper	pinch of paprika
100 g/4 oz cream cheese	½ cup cream cheese
50 g/2 oz butter	¼ cup butter
1 egg yolk	1 egg yolk
2 teaspoons water	2 teaspoons water
Filling	*Filling*
6 eggs	6 eggs
3 tablespoons milk	3 tablespoons milk
salt and pepper	salt and pepper
25 g/1 oz butter	2 tablespoons butter
8 canned artichoke hearts, chopped	8 canned artichoke hearts, chopped
Garnish	*Garnish*
parsley sprigs	parsley sprigs
lemon slices	lemon slices

Sift together the flour, salt and paprika. Rub (cut) in the cream cheese and butter then mix to a soft dough with the egg yolk and water.

Roll out the dough and line four 10 cm/4 inch round individual flan tins (pie pans). Line with greaseproof (parchment) paper and dried beans and 'bake blind' in a preheated moderately hot oven (200°C/400°F, Gas Mark 6) for 15 to 20 minutes until really crisp. Beat the eggs and milk together and season generously. Melt the butter in a pan and scramble the eggs lightly. Stir in the artichokes and spoon into the prepared pastry cases. Garnish with parsley and lemon.
Serves 4

LEEK FLAN (PIE)

METRIC/IMPERIAL	AMERICAN
shortcrust pastry, made with 225 g/8 oz flour (page 94)	pie pastry, made with 2 cups flour (page 94)
1 kg/2 lb leeks, trimmed	2 lb leeks, trimmed
50 g/2 oz butter	¼ cup butter
3 egg yolks	3 egg yolks
150 ml/¼ pint single cream	⅔ cup light cream
salt and pepper	salt and pepper
Garnish	*Garnish*
parsley sprigs	parsley sprigs

Roll out the pastry and line a 20 cm/8 inch flan ring on a baking sheet. Line with greaseproof (parchment) paper and dried beans and 'bake blind' in a preheated moderately hot oven (200°C/400°F, Gas Mark 6) for about 15 minutes. Remove the paper and beans.

Thinly slice the leeks, wash well and dry. Melt the butter in a pan and sauté the leeks until just tender. Spoon into the flan case (pie shell). Beat the egg yolks and cream together and add salt and pepper to taste; pour over the leeks. Cook in a moderately hot oven (190°C/375°F, Gas Mark 5) for about 25 minutes until the filling is set. Garnish with parsley sprigs.
Serves 4 to 6

Leek Flan (Pie); Egg and Artichoke Tartlet; Celery, Almond and Gruyère Flan (Pie)

CELERY, ALMOND AND GRUYÈRE FLAN (PIE)

METRIC/IMPERIAL	AMERICAN
shortcrust pastry, made with 350 g/12 oz flour (page 94)	pie pastry, made with 3 cups flour (page 94)
1 × 524 g/1 lb 3 oz can celery hearts, drained	1 × 1¼ lb can celery hearts, drained
2 eggs	2 eggs
300 ml/½ pint single cream	1¼ cups light cream
50 g/2 oz Gruyère cheese, grated	½ cup grated Gruyère cheese
25 g/1 oz Parmesan cheese, grated	¼ cup grated Parmesan cheese
salt and pepper	salt and pepper
3 tablespoons flaked almonds	3 tablespoons slivered almonds

Roll out the pastry on a lightly floured surface and line a 25 cm/10 inch flan tin (pie pan). Line with greaseproof (parchment) paper and dried beans and 'bake blind' in a preheated moderately hot oven (200°C/400°F, Gas Mark 6) for 15 minutes. Remove the paper and beans.

Cut the celery hearts in half and arrange in a cartwheel pattern over the bottom of the flan case (pie shell). Beat together the eggs, cream, cheeses and salt and pepper to taste and pour over the celery. Sprinkle with the almonds and cook in a moderate oven (180°C/350°F, Gas Mark 4) for 30 minutes.
Serves 6

CHEESE AND COURGETTE (ZUCCHINI) QUICHE

METRIC/IMPERIAL	AMERICAN
shortcrust pastry, made with 350 g/12 oz flour (page 94)	pie pastry made with 3 cups flour (page 94)
15 g/½ oz butter	1 tablespoon butter
1 medium onion, chopped	1 medium-size onion, chopped
450 g/1 lb courgettes, grated	1 lb zucchini, grated
2 eggs	2 eggs
4 tablespoons soured cream	4 tablespoons sour cream
4 tablespoons grated Gruyère cheese	4 tablespoons grated Gruyère cheese
salt and pepper	salt and pepper

Roll out the pastry and line a 25 cm/10 inch flan tin (pie pan). Line with greaseproof (parchment) paper and dried beans and 'bake blind' in a moderately hot oven (200°C/400°F, Gas Mark 6) for 15 minutes. Remove the paper and beans.

Meanwhile melt the butter in a pan and fry the onion until transparent. Add the courgettes (zucchini) and stir well for 1 minute. Spoon into the flan case (pie shell). Mix together the cream, cheese and salt and pepper to taste and pour over the courgettes (zucchini). Cook in a moderately hot oven (190°C/375°F, Gas Mark 5) for 25 to 30 minutes until set.
Serves 6 to 8

EGG MAYONNAISE FLAN (PIE)

METRIC/IMPERIAL	AMERICAN
Flan case	*Pie shell*
100 g/4 oz plain flour	1 cup all-purpose flour
pinch of salt	pinch of salt
50 g/2 oz butter or margarine	$\frac{1}{4}$ cup butter or margarine
4 teaspoons cold water	4 teaspoons cold water
Filling	*Filling*
4 eggs, hard-boiled	4 eggs, hard-cooked
4 spring onions, chopped	4 scallions, chopped
2 tomatoes, chopped	2 tomatoes, chopped
$1\frac{1}{2}$ tablespoons chopped gherkins	$1\frac{1}{2}$ tablespoons chopped gherkins
2 tablespoons chopped parsley	2 tablespoons chopped parsley
1 tablespoon capers	1 tablespoon capers
150 ml/$\frac{1}{4}$ pint mayonnaise	$\frac{2}{3}$ cup mayonnaise
salt and pepper	salt and pepper
Garnish	*Garnish*
2 eggs, hard-boiled	2 eggs, hard-cooked
parsley sprigs	parsley sprigs

Sift the flour and a pinch of salt into a large bowl. Rub (cut) in the butter or margarine until the mixture resembles fine breadcrumbs. Add the water and mix to a soft dough. Roll out on a lightly floured surface and line a 19 cm/7$\frac{1}{2}$ inch fluted flan tin (pie pan). Line with greaseproof (parchment) paper and dried beans and 'bake blind' in a preheated moderately hot oven (200°C/400°F, Gas Mark 6) for 20 to 25 minutes until cooked. Remove the paper and beans and leave to cool.

Roughly chop the 4 eggs and mix with the filling ingredients. Season to taste. Pile into the flan case (pie shell) and garnish with the eggs, cut into wedges, and parsley.
Serves 4 to 6

CREAMY MUSHROOM QUICHE

METRIC/IMPERIAL	AMERICAN
Flan case	*Pie shell*
200 g/7 oz plain flour	$1\frac{3}{4}$ cups all-purpose flour
pinch of salt	pinch of salt
1 teaspoon dried thyme	1 teaspoon dried thyme
90 g/3$\frac{1}{2}$ oz butter or margarine	7 tablespoons butter or margarine
7 teaspoons cold water	7 teaspoons water
Filling	*Filling*
25 g/1 oz butter	2 tablespoons butter
225 g/8 oz button mushrooms, sliced	2 cups sliced button mushrooms
1 egg plus 1 egg yolk	1 egg plus 1 egg yolk
150 ml/$\frac{1}{4}$ pint single cream	$\frac{2}{3}$ cup light cream
salt and pepper	salt and pepper
Garnish	*Garnish*
sprig of thyme	sprig of thyme
3 button mushrooms, sliced	3 button mushrooms, sliced

Sift the flour and salt into a bowl. Add the thyme and rub (cut) in the butter or margarine until the mixture resembles fine breadcrumbs. Add the water and mix to a soft dough. Roll out on a lightly floured surface and line a 21 cm/8$\frac{1}{2}$ inch fluted flan tin (pie pan). Line with greaseproof (parchment) paper and dried beans and 'bake blind' in a preheated moderately hot oven (200°C/400°F, Gas Mark 6) for 20 minutes. Remove the paper and beans.

Melt the butter in a pan and sauté the mushrooms over a high heat. Beat together the egg, egg yolk, cream and salt and pepper to taste. Stir in the mushrooms. Pour into the flan case (pie shell) and cook in a moderately hot oven (190°C/375°F, Gas Mark 5) for 30 to 35 minutes until just set but still creamy. Serve hot, garnished with a sprig of thyme and mushroom slices.
Serves 6

WHOLESOME SPINACH QUICHE

METRIC/IMPERIAL	AMERICAN
shortcrust pastry, made with 175 g/6 oz wholemeal flour (page 94)	pie pastry, made with $1\frac{1}{2}$ cups wholewheat flour (page 94)
2 eggs	2 eggs
1 × 225 g/8 oz packet frozen chopped spinach, thawed and well drained	1 × $\frac{1}{2}$ lb package frozen chopped spinach, thawed and well drained
1 medium onion, finely chopped	1 medium-size onion, finely chopped
50 g/2 oz Cheddar cheese, grated	$\frac{1}{2}$ cup grated Cheddar cheese
150 ml/$\frac{1}{4}$ pint single cream	$\frac{2}{3}$ cup light cream
grated nutmeg	grated nutmeg
salt and pepper	salt and pepper

Roll out the pastry on a lightly floured surface and line a 20 cm/8 inch flan tin (pie pan). Line with greaseproof (parchment) paper and dried beans and 'bake blind' in a preheated moderately hot oven (200°C/400°F, Gas Mark 6) for 15 minutes. Remove the paper and beans.

Beat together all the remaining ingredients with nutmeg and salt and pepper to taste and pour into the flan case (pie shell). Cook in a moderate oven (180°C/350°F, Gas Mark 4) for 25 to 30 minutes until the filling is firm in the centre. Serve warm.
Serves 4

TWO CHEESE QUICHE

METRIC/IMPERIAL	AMERICAN
shortcrust pastry, made with 225 g/8 oz flour (page 94)	pie pastry, made with 2 cups flour (page 94)
75 g/3 oz cheese (Roquefort or Dolcelatte)	3 oz cheese (Roquefort or Dolcellate)
175 g/6 oz cream cheese	$\frac{3}{4}$ cup cream cheese
2 eggs, beaten	2 eggs, beaten
150 ml/$\frac{1}{4}$ pint single cream	$\frac{2}{3}$ cup light cream
1 tablespoon chopped spring onion	1 tablespoon chopped scallions
salt and pepper	salt and pepper

Roll out the pastry and line a 20 cm/8 inch flan tin (pie pan). Line with greaseproof (parchment) paper and dried beans and 'bake blind' in a preheated hot oven (220°C/425°F, Gas Mark 7) for 10 minutes. Remove the paper and beans.

Beat together the cheeses and then gradually stir in the eggs, cream, spring onions (scallions) and salt and pepper to taste. Pour into the flan case (pie shell) and cook in a moderately hot oven (190°C/375°F, Gas Mark 5) for about 30 minutes. Serve at once.
Serves 4 to 6

Egg Mayonnaise Flan (Pie); Wholesome Spinach Quiche

HOT AVOCADO TARTS

METRIC/IMPERIAL	AMERICAN
Pastry	*Pie dough*
175 g/6 oz plain flour	1½ cups all-purpose flour
pinch of salt	pinch of salt
¼ teaspoon chilli powder	¼ teaspoon chili powder
75 g/3 oz butter or margarine	6 tablespoons butter or margarine
6 teaspoons cold water	6 teaspoons cold water
Filling	*Filling*
1 ripe avocado, peeled and stoned	1 ripe avocado, peeled and seeded
1 tablespoon finely chopped onion	1 tablespoon finely chopped onion
1 tablespoon finely chopped celery	1 tablespoon finely chopped celery
1 tablespoon lemon juice	1 tablespoon lemon juice
6 tablespoons soured cream	6 tablespoons sour cream
1 egg	1 egg
salt and pepper	salt and pepper
Garnish	*Garnish*
tomato wedges	tomato wedges
celery leaves	celery leaves

Sift the flour, salt and chilli powder together. Rub (cut) in the butter or margarine until the mixture resembles fine breadcrumbs. Add the water and mix to a soft dough. Roll out on a lightly floured surface and line four 10 cm/4 inch round individual fluted flan tins (pie pans). Line with greaseproof (parchment) paper and dried beans and 'bake blind' in a preheated moderately hot oven (200°C/400°F, Gas Mark 6) for 15 minutes. Remove the paper and beans.

Meanwhile mash the avocado and mix with the remaining filling ingredients. Spoon into the pastry case (pie shell) and cook in the moderately hot oven (200°C/400°F, Gas Mark 6) for a further 15 minutes. Serve warm, garnished with tomato wedges and celery leaves.
Serves 4

CRUNCHY CUCUMBER AND CHIVE TARTS

METRIC/IMPERIAL	AMERICAN
100 g/4 oz plain flour	1 cup all-purpose flour
pinch of mustard powder	pinch of dry mustard
75 g/3 oz butter	6 tablespoons butter
1 tablespoon beaten egg	1 tablespoon beaten egg
50 g/2 oz Cheddar cheese, grated	½ cup grated Cheddar cheese
Filling	*Filling*
25 g/1 oz butter	2 tablespoons butter
225 g/8 oz cucumber, peeled, seeded and diced	1 cup peeled, seeded and diced cucumber
1 tablespoon plain flour	1 tablespoon all-purpose flour
120 ml/4 fl oz milk	½ cup milk
1 tablespoon chopped chives	1 tablespoon chopped chives
salt and pepper	salt and pepper
Garnish	*Garnish*
lemon slices	lemon slices
chopped chives	chopped chives

Sift the flour and mustard together. Rub (cut) in the butter until the mixture resembles fine breadcrumbs. Stir in the egg and cheese and mix to a soft dough. Roll out on a lightly floured surface and line nine 6 cm/2½ inch fluted tins (pans). Prick the bases and 'bake blind' in a preheated moderately hot oven (200°C/400°F, Gas Mark 6) for 15 minutes until crisp and golden. Cool and carefully remove from the tins.

Meanwhile melt the butter in a pan and sauté the cucumber until just tender. Stir in the flour and cook for 1 minute. Gradually stir in the milk and chives and bring the sauce to the boil. Add salt and pepper to taste. Spoon into the prepared pastry cases (pie shells) and garnish with twisted lemon slices and chives.
Makes 9

MEXICAN FLAN (PIE)

METRIC/IMPERIAL

Flan case
100 g/4 oz plain flour
50 g/2 oz butter or
  margarine
1 teaspoon dried mixed
  herbs
pinch of salt
4 teaspoons cold water
Filling
1 tablespoon oil
1 red pepper, cored, seeded
  and chopped
1 green pepper, cored,
  seeded and chopped
4 spring onions, chopped
100 g/4 oz frozen sweetcorn
2 eggs
150 ml/¼ pint milk
¼ teaspoon Tabasco sauce

AMERICAN

Pie shell
1 cup all-purpose flour
¼ cup butter or margarine
1 teaspoon dried mixed
  herbs
pinch of salt
4 teaspoons cold water
Filling
1 tablespoon oil
1 red pepper, seeded and
  diced
1 green pepper, seeded and
  diced
4 scallions, chopped
¾ cup frozen whole kernel
  corn
2 eggs
⅔ cup milk
¼ teaspoon hot pepper sauce

Sift the flour into a mixing bowl and rub (cut) in the butter or margarine until the mixture resembles fine breadcrumbs. Add the herbs, salt and water and mix to a soft dough. Roll out on a lightly floured surface and line a 20 cm/8 inch flan tin (pie pan). Chill while preparing the filling.

Heat the oil in a pan and fry the peppers and spring onions (scallions) until just tender. Add the corn. Beat together the eggs, milk and Tabasco (hot pepper) sauce. Spoon the vegetables into the prepared flan case (pie shell) and pour in the egg mixture. Cook in a preheated moderately hot oven (190°C/375°F, Gas Mark 5) for 35 to 40 minutes until firmly set. Serve warm.

Serves 4 to 6

Mexican Flan (Pie); Hot Avocado Tart

FRENCH ONION FLAN (PIE)

METRIC/IMPERIAL	AMERICAN
175 g/6 oz frozen puff pastry, thawed	6 oz frozen puff pastry, thawed
25 g/1 oz butter	2 tablespoons butter
2 tablespoons oil	2 tablespoons oil
550 g/1¼ lb onions, thickly sliced	1¼ lb onions, thickly sliced
2 egg yolks	2 egg yolks
120 ml/4 fl oz double cream	½ cup heavy cream
¼ teaspoon ground nutmeg	¼ teaspoon ground nutmeg
salt and pepper	salt and pepper

Roll out the pastry on a lightly floured surface and line a 20 cm/8 inch flan tin (pie pan). Chill while preparing the filling.

Melt the butter and oil in a large saucepan and sauté the onions for 10 minutes, stirring occasionally until soft and golden. Beat together the egg yolks, cream, nutmeg and salt and pepper to taste. Add the onions and pour into the prepared pastry case. Cook in a preheated moderately hot oven (200°C/400°F, Gas Mark 6) for 20 to 25 minutes until the pastry is crisp and the filling is set. Serve warm.
Serves 4 to 6

CAULIFLOWER CHEESE AND WALNUT FLAN (PIE)

METRIC/IMPERIAL	AMERICAN
Flan case	*Pie shell*
100 g/4 oz plain flour	1 cup all-purpose flour
pinch of mustard powder	pinch of dry mustard
75 g/3 oz butter	6 tablespoons butter
50 g/2 oz Cheddar cheese, grated	½ cup grated Cheddar cheese
1 tablespoon beaten egg	1 tablespoon beaten egg
Filling	*Filling*
1 medium cauliflower, broken into florets	1 medium-size cauliflower, broken into florets
salt and pepper	salt and pepper
25 g/1 oz butter	2 tablespoons butter
25 g/1 oz plain flour	¼ cup all-purpose flour
150 ml/¼ pint milk	⅔ cup milk
100 g/4 oz Cheddar cheese, grated	1 cup grated Cheddar cheese
25 g/1 oz walnuts, coarsely chopped	¼ cup coarsely chopped walnuts

Sift the flour and mustard together. Rub (cut) in the butter until the mixture resembles fine breadcrumbs. Add the cheese and egg and mix to a soft dough. Roll out on a lightly floured surface and line a 20 cm/8 inch flan tin (pie pan). Line with greaseproof (parchment) paper and dried beans and 'bake blind' in a preheated moderately hot oven (200°C/400°F, Gas Mark 6) for 20 to 25 minutes until crisp.

Meanwhile cook the cauliflower florets in boiling salted water until just tender. Drain well, reserving 150 ml/¼ pint (⅔ cup) of the cooking water. Melt the butter in a pan, stir in the flour and cook for 1 minute. Gradually add the milk and reserved water and bring to the boil. Stir in half the cheese until melted. Add the cauliflower and mix to coat evenly. Spoon into the flan case, sprinkle with walnuts and the remaining cheese. Place under a hot grill (broiler) until golden.
Serves 4 to 6

ORIENTAL CARROT QUICHE

METRIC/IMPERIAL	AMERICAN
shortcrust pastry made with 175 g/6 oz flour (page 94)	pie pastry made with 1½ cups flour (page 94)
275 g/10 oz carrots, thickly sliced	10 oz carrots, thickly sliced
knob of butter	pat of butter
4 tablespoons water	¼ cup water
½ teaspoon sugar	½ teaspoon sugar
½ teaspoon ground cinnamon	½ teaspoon ground cinnamon
1 teaspoon mustard powder	1 teaspoon mustard powder
2 eggs	2 eggs
200 ml/⅓ pint milk	⅞ cup milk
salt and pepper	salt and pepper
Garnish	*Garnish*
chopped parsley	chopped parsley

Roll out the pastry on a lightly floured surface and line a 20 cm/8 inch flan tin (pie pan). Chill while preparing the filling.

Place the carrots, butter, water, sugar, cinnamon and mustard in a saucepan. Bring to the boil, cover and simmer for 10 minutes, shaking the pan occasionally. Beat the eggs and milk together and season generously with salt and pepper. Stir in the carrot mixture and spoon into the flan case (pie shell). Cook in a preheated moderate oven (190°C/375°F, Gas Mark 5) for 30 to 40 minutes. Garnish with parsley.
Serves 4 to 6

FENNEL AND POTATO FLAN (PIE)

METRIC/IMPERIAL	AMERICAN
Flan case	*Pie shell*
50 g/2 oz instant potato powder	½ cup instant potato powder
50 g/2 oz plain flour	½ cup all-purpose flour
50 g/2 oz butter	¼ cup butter
1 egg yolk	1 egg yolk
2 teaspoons iced water	2 teaspoons iced water
Filling	*Filling*
25 g/1 oz butter	2 tablespoons butter
225 g/8 oz fennel, chopped	2 cups chopped fennel
2 eggs	2 eggs
150 ml/¼ pint single cream	⅔ cup light cream
salt and pepper	salt and pepper
squeeze of lemon juice	dash of lemon juice
Garnish	*Garnish*
fennel sprigs	fennel sprigs

Mix together the instant potato powder and flour in a bowl and rub (cut) in the butter. Add the egg yolk and water and mix to a soft dough. Roll out on a lightly floured surface and line a 20 cm/8 inch flan tin (pie pan). Line with greaseproof (parchment) paper and dried beans and 'bake blind' in a moderately hot oven (200°C/400°F, Gas Mark 6) for 15 minutes. Remove the paper and beans.

Melt the butter and sauté the fennel until just tender. Beat the eggs and cream together and add salt, pepper and lemon juice to taste. Stir in the fennel. Pour the mixture into the flan case (pie shell) and cook in a moderately hot oven (200°C/400°F, Gas Mark 6) for 25 minutes. Garnish with fennel.
Serves 4 to 6

French Onion Flan (Pie); Oriental Carrot Quiche; Cauliflower Cheese and Walnut Flan (Pie)

SAVOURY CHEESECAKES

With their crisp savoury bases and contrasting creamy textures, these cheesecakes are luxurious dishes to serve at parties. This chapter contains ideas for appetizers, main courses and even substitutes for the biscuits-and-cheese course.

GUACAMOLE CHEESECAKE

METRIC/IMPERIAL	AMERICAN
Base	*Base*
100 g/4 oz taco chips or potato crisps, finely crushed	1 cup finely crushed taco or corn chips
50 g/2 oz butter, melted	$\frac{1}{4}$ cup butter, melted
Filling	*Filling*
1 × 225 g/8 oz packet cream cheese	1 × $\frac{1}{2}$ lb package cream cheese
2 eggs, separated	2 eggs, separated
5 tablespoons mayonnaise	5 tablespoons mayonnaise
2 ripe avocados, peeled and stoned	2 ripe avocados, peeled and seeded
juice of $\frac{1}{2}$ large lemon	juice of $\frac{1}{2}$ large lemon
2 tablespoons tomato-based chilli sauce	2 tablespoons tomato-based chili sauce
1 tablespoon tomato purée	1 tablespoon tomato paste
Tabasco sauce	hot pepper sauce
salt and pepper	salt and pepper
1 envelope gelatine	1 envelope unflavored gelatin
5 tablespoons water	5 tablespoons water
Garnish	*Garnish*
1 medium tomato	1 medium-size tomato
stoned black olives	pitted black olives

Mix together the taco chips and butter and press over the bottom of a greased 18 to 20 cm/7 to 8 inch loose-bottomed cake tin (spring form pan). Chill until set.

Meanwhile beat the cream cheese with the egg yolks and mayonnaise until smooth. Mash the avocados with the lemon juice and beat into the cheese mixture with the chilli sauce, tomato purée (paste), Tabasco (hot pepper) sauce, and salt and pepper to taste. Put the gelatine and water into a small heatproof bowl over a saucepan of hot water and stir until the gelatine has dissolved. Mix the gelatine thoroughly into the avocado mixture. Chill until the mixture is beginning to thicken, then beat the egg whites until stiff and fold them in.

Spoon the avocado mixture on top of the taco base and smooth the top. Chill until the filling is set.

Remove the cheesecake from the tin. Halve the tomato and scoop out all the seeds and membrane. Cut the tomato into strips and arrange decoratively on top of the cheesecake with the olives, sliced if liked.

Serves 6 to 8 as an appetizer

LAYERED SALMON CHEESECAKE RING

METRIC/IMPERIAL	AMERICAN
100 g/4 oz water biscuits, finely crushed	1 cup finely crushed water biscuits or saltine crackers
50 g/2 oz butter, melted	$\frac{1}{4}$ cup butter, melted
Top layer	*Top layer*
1 × 75 g/3 oz packet cream cheese	1 × 3 oz package cream cheese
2 tablespoons mayonnaise	2 tablespoons mayonnaise
1 tablespoon lemon juice	1 tablespoon lemon juice
2 envelopes gelatine	2 envelopes unflavored gelatin
5 tablespoons water	5 tablespoons water
Bottom layer	*Bottom layer*
1 × 200 g/7 oz can red salmon, drained and flaked	1 can (8 oz) red salmon, drained and flaked
$\frac{1}{4}$ cucumber, peeled and diced	$\frac{1}{4}$ cucumber, peeled and diced
1 celery stalk, diced	1 celery stalk, diced
2 spring onions, chopped	2 scallions, chopped
6 tablespoons mayonnaise	6 tablespoons mayonnaise
salt and pepper	salt and pepper

For the top layer, beat the cream cheese with the mayonnaise and lemon juice until smooth. Put the gelatine and water into a small heatproof bowl over a pan of hot water and stir until the gelatine has dissolved. Add half the gelatine to the cheese mixture and combine thoroughly. (Keep the remaining gelatine liquid in the bowl over hot water.) Pour the cheese mixture into a dampened 20 to 23 cm/8 to 9 inch ring mould and spread out evenly. Chill until set.

For the bottom layer, mix together all the ingredients with salt and pepper to taste. Add the remaining gelatine and combine thoroughly. Spoon into the tin on top of the set cheese layer.

Mix together the biscuits (or crackers) and butter and press lightly but firmly over the salmon layer in the mould. Chill until set. Unmould so that the crumb base is on the bottom.
Serves 4 to 6 as an appetizer

PRAWN (SHRIMP) COCKTAIL CHEESECAKE

METRIC/IMPERIAL	AMERICAN
Base	*Base*
100 g/4 oz rye or wholemeal diet crackers, finely crushed	1 cup finely crushed rye or wholewheat diet crackers
50 g/2 oz butter, melted	$\frac{1}{4}$ cup butter, melted
Filling	*Filling*
1 × 225 g/8 oz packet cream cheese	1 × $\frac{1}{2}$ lb package cream cheese
2 eggs, separated	2 eggs, separated
5 tablespoons mayonnaise	5 tablespoons mayonnaise
3–5 tablespoons tomato-based chilli sauce	3–5 tablespoons tomato-based chili sauce
$\frac{1}{2}$ teaspoon grated lemon rind	$\frac{1}{2}$ teaspoon grated lemon rind
1 teaspoon lemon juice	1 teaspoon lemon juice
salt and pepper	salt and pepper
1 envelope gelatine	1 envelope unflavored gelatin
5 tablespoons water	5 tablespoons water
100 g/4 oz cooked peeled prawns, chopped	1 cup chopped cooked shelled shrimp
Garnish	*Garnish*
unpeeled prawns	unshelled jumbo shrimp
dill sprigs	dill sprigs

Mix together the crackers and butter and press over the bottom of a greased 18 to 20 cm/7 to 8 inch loose-bottomed cake tin (springform pan). Chill until set.

Meanwhile beat the cream cheese with the egg yolks and mayonnaise until smooth. Add the chilli sauce, lemon rind and juice and salt and pepper to taste and mix well. Put the gelatine and water into a small heatproof bowl over a pan of hot water and stir until dissolved. Mix the gelatine thoroughly into the cheese mixture. Fold in the chopped prawns (shrimp). Chill until the mixture is beginning to thicken, then beat the egg whites until stiff and fold them in.

Spoon the prawn (shrimp) mixture into the pan on top of the crumb base and smooth the top. Chill until the filling is set.

Remove the cheesecake from the pan and garnish with prawns and dill sprigs.
Serves 6 to 8 as an appetizer

HAM AND VEGETABLE CHEESECAKE

METRIC/IMPERIAL	AMERICAN
Base	*Base*
100 g/4 oz biscuits for cheese, finely crushed	1 cup finely crushed crackers for cheese
50 g/2 oz butter, melted	¼ cup butter, melted
Filling	*Filling*
25 g/1 oz butter	2 tablespoons butter
100 g/4 oz mushrooms, sliced	1 cup sliced mushrooms
75–100 g/3–4 oz cooked vegetables such as green beans, cabbage, carrots, etc., chopped	¾ cup chopped cooked vegetables such as green beans, cabbage, carrots, etc.
100 g/4 oz cooked ham, diced	½ cup diced cooked ham
1 × 225 g/8 oz packet cream cheese	1 × ½ lb package cream cheese
225 g/8 oz cottage cheese, sieved	1 cup sieved cottage cheese
3 eggs, separated	3 eggs, separated
75 g/3 oz Cheddar cheese, grated	¾ cup grated Cheddar cheese
½ teaspoon dried thyme	½ teaspoon dried thyme
salt and pepper	salt and pepper

Mix together the biscuits (crackers) and butter and press over the bottom of a greased 18 to 20 cm/7 to 8 inch loose-bottomed cake tin (springform pan). Chill until set.

Meanwhile melt the butter in a frying pan. Add the mushrooms and fry until golden brown. Stir in the vegetables and ham. Remove from the heat and drain off any excess liquid.

Beat the cream and cottage cheeses with the egg yolks until smooth. Add the Cheddar cheese, ham mixture, thyme and salt and pepper to taste and mix well. Beat the egg whites until stiff and fold into the mixture.

Spoon into the cake pan on top of the crumb base and smooth the top. Cook in a preheated moderate oven (160°C/325°F, Gas Mark 3) for 1 to 1¼ hours or until the filling is just set and the top golden brown. Leave to cool in the pan before serving warm or at room temperature.

Serves 6 to 8

MEXICAN CORN CHEESECAKE

METRIC/IMPERIAL	AMERICAN
Base	*Base*
75 g/3 oz yellow corn meal	½ cup yellow corn meal
50 g/2 oz plain flour	½ cup all-purpose flour
2 teaspoons baking powder	2 teaspoons baking powder
¼ teaspoon ground cumin	¼ teaspoon ground cumin
¼ teaspoon salt	¼ teaspoon salt
6 tablespoons milk	6 tablespoons milk
1 egg, beaten	1 egg, beaten
25 g/1 oz butter, melted	2 tablespoons butter, melted
Filling	*Filling*
2 tablespoons oil	2 tablespoons oil
1 large onion, finely chopped	1 large onion, finely chopped
1 green pepper, cored, seeded and finely chopped	1 green pepper, seeded and finely chopped
1 × 225 g/8 oz packet cream cheese	1 × ½ lb package cream cheese
3 eggs, separated	3 eggs, separated
100 g/4 oz Cheddar cheese, grated	1 cup grated Cheddar or Monterey Jack cheese
1 × 198 g/7 oz can sweetcorn kernels, drained	1 × ½ lb can whole kernel corn, drained
1 teaspoon dried oregano	1 teaspoon dried oregano
Tabasco sauce	hot pepper sauce
salt and pepper	salt and pepper
Garnish	*Garnish*
1 small onion, sliced into rings	1 small onion, sliced into rings
1 green pepper, cored, seeded and sliced into rings	1 green pepper, seeded and sliced into rings

Place the corn meal in a bowl and sift in the flour, baking powder, cumin and salt. Add the milk, egg and butter and beat until fairly smooth. Spoon into a greased 18 to 20 cm/7 to 8 inch loose-bottomed cake tin (springform pan) and spread evenly over the bottom and about 2.5 cm/1 inch up the sides.

Heat the oil in a frying pan. Add the onion and green pepper and fry until softened. Remove from the heat and drain off any excess oil. Beat the cream cheese with the egg yolks until smooth. Add the fried vegetables, Cheddar cheese, corn, oregano and Tabasco sauce with salt and pepper to taste and mix well. Beat the egg whites until stiff and fold into the mixture.

Spoon into the cake pan on top of the corn meal base. Cook in a preheated moderate oven (160°C/325°F, Gas Mark 3) for 1 to 1¼ hours or until the filling is just set golden brown. Leave to cool in the pan and serve warm or at room temperature. Garnish with onion and green pepper rings.

Serves 6 to 8

Ham and Vegetable Cheesecake; Mexican Corn Cheesecake

PIZZA CHEESECAKE

METRIC/IMPERIAL	AMERICAN
shortcrust pastry made with 100 g/4 oz plain flour (p. 94)	pie pastry made with 1 cup all-purpose flour (page 94)
2 tablespoons olive oil	2 tablespoons olive oil
1 onion, finely chopped	1 onion, finely chopped
1 clove garlic, crushed	1 clove garlic, crushed
1 green pepper, cored, seeded and diced	1 green pepper, seeded and diced
450 g/1 lb ricotta cheese	2 cups ricotta cheese
3 eggs, separated	3 eggs, separated
100 g/4 oz Romano or pecorino cheese, grated	1 cup grated Romano or pecorino cheese
1 teaspoon dried herbs	1 teaspoon dried herbs
salt and pepper	salt and pepper
Topping	*Topping*
50 g/2 oz garlic sausage, thinly sliced and halved	2 oz garlic sausage, thinly sliced and halved
1 small tomato, sliced	1 small tomato, sliced
6 black olives, halved	6 ripe olives, halved
1 tablespoon grated Romano or pecorino cheese	1 tablespoon grated Romano or pecorino cheese

Roll out the dough on a floured surface and line the bottom of a greased 18 to 20 cm/7 to 8 inch loose-bottomed cake tin (springform pan). Prick the dough all over with a fork, then cook in a preheated moderately hot oven (190°C/375°F, Gas Mark 5) for 15 to 20 minutes or until lightly browned.

Meanwhile heat the oil in a frying pan. Add the onion, garlic and green pepper and fry until softened. Remove from the heat and drain off all excess liquid.

Beat the ricotta cheese with the egg yolks until smooth. Add the Romano cheese, fried vegetables, herbs and salt and pepper to taste and mix well. Beat the egg whites until stiff and fold into the mixture.

Spoon into the pan on top of the pastry base and smooth the top. Bake for 45 minutes then arrange the sausage, tomato and olives decoratively on the top. Sprinkle with cheese. Return to the oven, reduce the temperature to moderate (160°C/325°F, Gas Mark 3) and cook for 1 to 1¼ hours or until the filling is set. Leave to cool in the pan before serving warm or at room temperature.
Serves 6 to 8

Pizza Cheesecake; Spinach Cheesecake

HOT TUNA CHEESECAKE

METRIC/IMPERIAL	AMERICAN
Base	*Base*
100 g/4 oz snack biscuits, finely crushed	1 cup finely crushed snack crackers
50 g/2 oz butter, melted	$\frac{1}{4}$ cup butter, melted
Filling	*Filling*
1 × 225 g/8 oz packet cream cheese	1 × $\frac{1}{2}$ lb package cream cheese
3 eggs, separated	3 eggs, separated
1 × 200 g/7 oz can tuna fish, drained and flaked	1 × $\frac{1}{2}$ lb can tuna fish, drained and flaked
100 g/4 oz Cheddar cheese, grated	1 cup grated Cheddar cheese
4 tablespoons mayonnaise	$\frac{1}{4}$ cup mayonnaise
3 spring onions, chopped	3 scallions, chopped
4 tablespoons chopped canned pimiento	$\frac{1}{4}$ cup chopped canned pimiento
1 tablespoon white wine vinegar	1 tablespoon white wine vinegar
salt and pepper	salt and pepper

Mix together the biscuits (crackers) and butter and press over the bottom of a greased 18 to 20 cm/7 to 8 inch loose-bottomed cake tin (springform pan). Chill until set.

Meanwhile beat the cream cheese with the egg yolks until smooth. Add the remaining ingredients, with salt and pepper to taste, and mix well. Beat the egg whites until stiff and fold into the mixture.

Spoon into the cake pan on top of the crumb base and smooth the top. Cook in a preheated moderate oven (160°C/325°F, Gas Mark 3) for 1¼ to 1½ hours or until the filling is just set and the top nicely browned. Leave to cool in the pan before serving warm or at room temperature.
Serves 6 to 8

SPINACH CHEESECAKE

METRIC/IMPERIAL	AMERICAN
shortcrust pastry made with 100 g/4 oz flour (page 94)	pie pastry made with 1 cup flour (page 94)
25 g/1 oz butter	2 tablespoons butter
1 onion, finely chopped	1 onion, finely chopped
1 clove garlic, crushed	1 clove garlic, crushed
1 × 300 g/10 oz packet frozen chopped spinach, thawed and well drained	1 × 10 oz package frozen chopped spinach, thawed and well drained
$\frac{1}{4}$ teaspoon dried basil	$\frac{1}{4}$ teaspoon dried basil
$\frac{1}{4}$ teaspoon dried marjoram	$\frac{1}{4}$ teaspoon dried marjoram
$\frac{1}{4}$ teaspoon dried thyme	$\frac{1}{4}$ teaspoon dried thyme
1 × 225 g/8 oz packet cream cheese	1 × $\frac{1}{2}$ lb package cream cheese
3 eggs, separated	3 eggs, separated
100 g/4 oz Gruyère cheese, grated	1 cup grated Gruyère or Swiss cheese
salt and pepper	salt and pepper
milk or single cream if necessary	milk or light cream if necessary
Topping	*Topping*
25 g/1 oz Parmesan cheese, freshly grated	$\frac{1}{4}$ cup freshly grated Parmesan cheese
2 tablespoons dry breadcrumbs	2 tablespoons dry bread crumbs

Roll out the dough on a floured surface and use to line the bottom of a greased 18 to 20 cm/7 to 8 inch loose-bottomed cake tin (springform pan). Prick the dough all over with a fork, then cook in a preheated moderately hot oven (190°C/375°F, Gas Mark 5) for 15 to 20 minutes or until lightly browned.

Meanwhile melt the butter in a frying pan. Add the onion and garlic and fry until softened. Stir in the spinach and herbs and fry for a further 3 minutes. Remove from the heat and drain off excess liquid.

Beat the cream cheese with the egg yolks until smooth. Add the Gruyère cheese, spinach mixture and salt and pepper to taste and mix well. If the mixture is very stiff, soften it slightly with a little milk or cream. Beat the egg whites until stiff and fold into the mixture.

Spoon into the cake pan on top of the pastry base and smooth the top. Return to the oven, reduce the temperature to moderate (160°C/325°F, Gas Mark 3) and cook for 45 minutes.

Mix the Parmesan cheese with the breadcrumbs and sprinkle over the top of the cheesecake. Cook for a further 15 to 30 minutes or until the filling is just set and the top golden brown. Serve warm or at room temperature.
Serves 6 to 8

COTTAGE CHEESECAKE

METRIC/IMPERIAL	AMERICAN
Base	*Base*
75 g/3 oz plain flour	$\frac{3}{4}$ cup all-purpose flour
pinch of salt	pinch of salt
50 g/2 oz butter	$\frac{1}{4}$ cup butter
50 g/2 oz cottage cheese, sieved	$\frac{1}{4}$ cup sieved cottage cheese
Filling	*Filling*
225 g/8 oz cottage cheese, sieved	1 cup sieved cottage cheese
3 eggs, separated	3 eggs, separated
150 ml/$\frac{1}{4}$ pint soured cream	$\frac{2}{3}$ cup sour cream
225 g/8 oz cooked ham, diced	1 cup diced cooked ham
1 large celery stalk, diced	1 large celery stalk, diced
4 spring onions, chopped	4 scallions, chopped
100 g/4 oz Gruyère cheese, grated	1 cup grated Gruyère or Swiss cheese
1 tablespoon sweetcorn relish	1 tablespoon corn relish
pinch of cayenne pepper	pinch of cayenne
salt and pepper	salt and pepper
Garnish	*Garnish*
chopped chives	chopped chives

Sift the flour and salt into a bowl. Rub (cut) in the butter until the mixture resembles breadcrumbs. Add the cottage cheese and mix to a smooth dough. Press the dough over the bottom of a greased 18 to 20 cm/7 to 8 inch loose-bottomed cake tin (springform pan). Prick with a fork, then cook in a preheated moderate oven (190°C/375°F, Gas Mark 5) for 15 to 20 minutes.

Meanwhile beat the cottage cheese with the egg yolks until smooth. Add the remaining filling ingredients, with salt and pepper to taste, and mix well. Beat the egg whites until stiff and fold into the mixture.

Spoon into the pan on top of the pastry base and smooth the top. Return to the oven, reduce the temperature to moderate (160°C/325°F, Gas Mark 3) and cook for 1¼ to 1½ hours or until the filling is just set and the top golden brown. Serve warm or at room temperature, garnished with chopped chives.
Serves 6 to 8

GREEN BEAN AND BACON CHEESECAKE

METRIC/IMPERIAL	AMERICAN
shortcrust pastry made with 100 g/4 oz plain flour (page 94)	pie pastry made with 1 cup all-purpose flour (page 94)
6 streaky bacon rashers, rinds removed	6 bacon slices
1 small onion, finely chopped	1 small onion, finely chopped
1 clove garlic, crushed	1 clove garlic, crushed
100 g/4 oz green beans, chopped	1 cup chopped green beans
1 × 225 g/8 oz packet cream cheese	1 × $\frac{1}{2}$ lb package cream cheese
3 eggs, separated	3 eggs, separated
225 g/8 oz Cheddar cheese, grated	2 cups grated Cheddar cheese
salt and pepper	salt and pepper
25 g/1 oz Parmesan cheese, freshly grated	$\frac{1}{4}$ cup freshly grated Parmesan cheese

Roll out the dough on a floured surface and line the bottom of a greased 18 to 20 cm/7 to 8 inch loose-bottomed cake tin (springform pan). Prick the dough all over, then cook in a preheated moderately hot oven (190°C/375°F, Gas Mark 5) for 15 to 20 minutes or until lightly browned.

Meanwhile fry the bacon in a frying pan until crisp and browned. Remove with tongs and drain on kitchen paper towels. Add the onion, garlic and beans to the bacon fat in the pan and fry until the onion is softened. Remove from the heat and drain off all excess fat and liquid.

Beat the cream cheese with the egg yolks until smooth. Add the Cheddar cheese and fried vegetables, season and mix well. Beat the egg whites until stiff and fold them in.

Spoon into the cake pan on top of the pastry base and smooth the top. Return to the oven, reduce the temperature to moderate (160°C/325°F, Gas Mark 3) and cook for 1 hour.

Crumble the fried bacon and mix with the Parmesan cheese. Sprinkle over the top of the cheesecake and cook for a further 15 minutes or until set and lightly browned.
Serves 6 to 8

ARTICHOKE AND SALAMI CHEESECAKE

METRIC/IMPERIAL	AMERICAN
100 g/4 oz biscuits for cheese, finely crushed	1 cup finely crushed crackers for cheese
50 g/2 oz butter, melted	$\frac{1}{4}$ cup butter, melted
225 g/8 oz ricotta cheese or sieved cottage cheese	1 cup ricotta cheese or sieved cottage cheese
3 eggs, separated	3 eggs, separated
175 g/6 oz mozzarella cheese, grated	6 oz mozzarella cheese, shredded (about 1$\frac{1}{2}$ cups)
100 g/4 oz Parmesan cheese, freshly grated	1 cup freshly grated Parmesan cheese
1 × 400 g/14 oz can artichoke hearts, drained and chopped	1 × 1 lb can artichoke hearts, drained and chopped
75 g/3 oz salami, chopped	$\frac{1}{2}$ cup chopped salami
$\frac{1}{2}$ teaspoon dried basil	$\frac{1}{2}$ teaspoon dried basil
$\frac{1}{2}$ teaspoon dried oregano	$\frac{1}{2}$ teaspoon dried oregano
$\frac{1}{2}$ teaspoon dried rosemary	$\frac{1}{2}$ teaspoon dried rosemary
salt and pepper	salt and pepper
Garnish	*Garnish*
3–4 slices salami, halved	3–4 slices salami, halved
watercress sprigs	watercress sprigs

Mix together the biscuits (crackers) and butter and press over the bottom of a greased 18 to 20 cm/7 to 8 inch loose-bottomed cake tin (springform pan). Chill until set.

Meanwhile beat the ricotta cheese with the egg yolks until smooth. Add the mozzarella cheese, two-thirds of the Parmesan cheese, the artichoke hearts, salami, herbs and salt and pepper to taste and mix well. Beat the egg whites until stiff and fold into the mixture.

Spoon into the pan on top of the crumb base and smooth the top. Cook in a preheated moderate oven (160°C/325°F, Gas Mark 3) for 45 minutes, then sprinkle over the remaining Parmesan cheese. Continue baking for 30 to 45 minutes or until the filling is set and the top nicely browned. Leave to cool in the pan before serving warm or at room temperature. Garnish with salami slices, rolled into cones, and watercress.
Serves 6 to 8

Green Bean and Bacon Cheesecake; Italian Three-Cheese Cheesecake

ITALIAN THREE-CHEESE CHEESECAKE

METRIC/IMPERIAL	AMERICAN
shortcrust pastry made with 100 g/4 oz plain flour (page 94)	pie pastry made with 1 cup all-purpose flour (page 94)
2 tablespoons olive oil	2 tablespoons olive oil
1 large onion, finely chopped	1 large onion, finely chopped
1 clove garlic, crushed	1 clove garlic, crushed
450 g/1 lb ricotta cheese or sieved cottage cheese	2 cups ricotta cheese or sieved cottage cheese
25 g/1 oz Parmesan cheese, freshly grated	$\frac{1}{4}$ cup freshly grated Parmesan cheese
3 eggs, beaten	3 eggs, beaten
175–225 g/6–8 oz mozzarella cheese, grated	6–8 oz mozzarella cheese, shredded (about $1\frac{1}{2}$–2 cups)
1 teaspoon dried Italian seasoning herbs	1 teaspoon dried Italian seasoning herbs
salt and pepper	salt and pepper

Roll out the dough on a floured surface and line the bottom of a greased 18 to 20 cm/7 to 8 inch loose-bottomed cake tin (springform pan). Prick the dough all over with a fork, then cook in a preheated moderately hot oven (190°C/375°F, Gas Mark 5) for 15 to 20 minutes or until lightly browned.

Meanwhile heat the oil in a frying pan. Add the onion and garlic and fry until softened. Remove from the heat and drain.

Beat the ricotta cheese, Parmesan cheese and eggs together until smooth. Add half the mozzarella cheese, the fried onion and garlic and the herbs. Season and mix well.

Spoon the cheese mixture into the pan over the pastry base and smooth the top. Sprinkle over the remaining mozzarella cheese. Return to the oven, reduce the temperature to moderate (160°C/325°F, Gas Mark 3) and cook for 1 to $1\frac{1}{4}$ hours or until the filling is set and golden brown on top. Leave to cool in the pan before serving warm or at room temperature.
Serves 8 to 10

PIQUANT CHEDDAR CHEESECAKE

METRIC/IMPERIAL	AMERICAN
shortcrust pastry made with 100 g/4 oz plain flour (page 94)	pie pastry made with 1 cup all-purpose flour (page 94)
2 × 225 g/8 oz packets cream cheese	2 × $\frac{1}{2}$ lb packages (8 oz each) cream cheese
3 eggs, beaten	3 eggs, beaten
450 g/1 lb mature Cheddar cheese, grated	1 lb sharp Cheddar cheese, grated (about 4 cups)
2 tablespoons chopped canned pimiento	2 tablespoons chopped canned pimiento
3 tablespoons finely chopped green pepper	3 tablespoons finely chopped green pepper
3 tablespoons finely chopped onion	3 tablespoons finely chopped onion
2 teaspoons Worcestershire sauce	2 teaspoons Worcestershire sauce
1 teaspoon Dijon mustard	1 teaspoon Dijon-style mustard
pinch of cayenne pepper	pinch of cayenne
salt and pepper	salt and pepper
Garnish	*Garnish*
sliced gherkins	sliced gherkins
strips of canned pimiento	strips of canned pimiento

Roll out the dough on a floured surface and use to line the bottom of a greased 18 to 20 cm/7 to 8 inch loose-bottomed cake tin (springform pan). Prick the dough all over with a fork, then cook in a preheated moderately hot oven (190°C/375°F, Gas Mark 5) for 15 to 20 minutes or until lightly browned.

Meanwhile beat the cream cheese with the eggs until smooth. Add the remaining ingredients, with salt and pepper to taste, and mix well.

Spoon the cheese mixture into the pan over the pastry base and smooth the top. Return to the oven, reduce the temperature to moderate (180°C/350°F, Gas Mark 4) and cook for 40 to 45 minutes or until the filling is set. Leave to cool in the pan before serving, garnished with gherkins and pimiento.
Serves 12

PARTY WALNUT BRIE CAKE

METRIC/IMPERIAL	AMERICAN
100 g/4 oz butter, melted	$\frac{1}{2}$ cup butter, melted
1 × 1 kg/2 lb whole plain or pepper Brie	1 (2 lb) whole plain or pepper Brie
225 g/8 oz water biscuits, crushed	2 cups crushed water biscuits or saltine crackers
25 g/1 oz walnuts, finely chopped	$\frac{1}{4}$ cup finely chopped walnuts
salt and pepper	salt and pepper
100 g/4 oz walnut halves	1 cup walnut halves

Use 25 g/1 oz (2 tablespoons) of the butter to grease a 25 to 28 cm/10 to 11 inch flan or quiche dish. Place the whole Brie in the dish.

Mix together the remaining butter, the crushed biscuits (or crackers), chopped walnuts and salt and pepper to taste. Sprinkle over the top of the cheese and press down lightly. Arrange the walnut halves over the top and press into the cheese.

Cook in a preheated moderate oven (180°C/350°F, Gas Mark 4) for 15 to 20 minutes or until heated through. Serve piping hot. The cake cannot be cut, but should be scooped out with a spoon.
Serves 20 to 24

HERBED CHEESECAKE

METRIC/IMPERIAL	AMERICAN
shortcrust pastry made with 100 g/4 oz plain flour (page 00)	pie pastry made with 1 cup all-purpose flour (page 00)
3 × 225 g/8 oz packets cream cheese	3 packages (8 oz each) cream cheese
3 eggs, beaten	3 eggs, beaten
2 cloves garlic, crushed	2 cloves garlic, crushed
1 teaspoon grated lemon rind	1 teaspoon grated lemon rind
3 tablespoons lemon juice	3 tablespoons lemon juice
3 tablespoons chopped mixed fresh herbs (chives, parsley, basil, thyme, marjoram)	3 tablespoons chopped mixed fresh herbs (chives, parsley, basil, thyme, marjoram)
salt and pepper	salt and pepper
parsley or basil sprig to garnish	parsley or basil sprig for garnish

Roll out the dough on a floured surface and use to line the bottom of a greased 18 to 20 cm/7 to 8 inch loose-bottomed cake tin (springform pan). Prick the dough all over with a fork, then cook in a preheated moderately hot oven (190°C/375°F Gas Mark 5) for 15 to 20 minutes or until lightly browned.

Meanwhile beat the cream cheese with the eggs until smooth. Beat in the garlic, lemon rind and juice, chopped herbs and salt and pepper to taste.

Spoon the cheese mixture into the pan over the pastry base and smooth the top. Return to the oven, reduce the temperature to moderate (160°C/325°F, Gas Mark 3) and cook for 1 to 1$\frac{1}{4}$ hours or until the filling is set. Leave to cool in the pan before serving, at room temperature, garnished with a sprig of parsley or basil.
Serves 12 to 16

Note: this cheesecake is delicious served after dinner instead of cheese and biscuits.

AFTER DINNER CHEESECAKE

METRIC/IMPERIAL	AMERICAN
100 g/4 oz water biscuits, finely crushed	1 cup finely crushed water biscuits or saltine crackers
50 g/2 oz butter, melted	$\frac{1}{4}$ cup butter, melted
1 × 225 g/8 oz packet cream cheese	1 × $\frac{1}{2}$ lb package cream cheese
3 eggs, beaten	3 eggs, beaten
450 g/1 lb goat's cheese, rind removed (if any)	1 lb goat's cheese, rind removed (if any)
Garnish	*Garnish*
watercress sprigs	watercress sprigs
radish slices	radish slices

Mix together the biscuits (or crackers) and butter and press over the bottom of a greased 18 to 20 cm/7 to 8 inch loose-bottomed cake tin (springform pan). Chill until set.

Meanwhile beat the cream cheese with the eggs until smooth. Beat in the goat's cheese.

Spoon the cheese mixture into the pan over the biscuit base and smooth the top. Cook in a preheated moderate oven (180°C/350°F, Gas Mark 4) for 35 to 40 minutes or until the filling is set and lightly browned. Leave to cool in the pan before serving, at room temperature, garnished with watercress and radish.

Serves 12 to 16

PEPPERED CAMEMBERT PIE

METRIC/IMPERIAL	AMERICAN
1 × 200 g/7 oz packet frozen puff pastry, thawed	1 × $\frac{1}{2}$ lb package frozen puff pastry, thawed
1 × 225–275 g/8–10 oz whole Camembert	1 (8–10 oz) whole Camembert
freshly ground black pepper	freshly ground black pepper
beaten egg to glaze	beaten egg to glaze

Divide the pastry dough in half. Roll out one half on a floured surface to a 20 cm/8 inch round. Place the cheese in the centre and sprinkle it generously with pepper. Roll out the remaining dough to a 20 cm/8 inch round and place on top of the cheese. Brush the edges with beaten egg and press together to seal. Make two or three slashes in the top layer of dough and place the pie on a greased baking sheet.

Brush all over with beaten egg, then cook in a preheated hot oven (230°C/450°F, Gas Mark 8) for 15 minutes or until the pastry is puffed and golden. Serve piping hot.

Serves 6 to 8

Note: this cheesecake is delicious served after dinner instead of cheese and biscuits.

Herbed Cheesecake; Peppered Camembert Pie

CALORIE CONSCIOUS CHEESECAKES AND FLANS

Not all cheesecake and flan recipes require temptingly fattening ingredients. This chapter gives inventive and delicious recipes for savoury and sweet dishes which are low in calories.

MIXED VEGETABLE FLAN (PIE)

METRIC/IMPERIAL	AMERICAN
Flan case	*Pie shell*
750 g/1½ lb potatoes	1½ lb potatoes
salt and pepper	salt and pepper
Filling	*Filling*
1 stick celery, chopped	1 celery stalk, chopped
2 carrots, diced	2 carrots, diced
100 g/4 oz cauliflower florets	¼ lb cauliflower florets
100 g/4 oz peas	¾ cup peas
100 g/4 oz beans, cut into 2.5 cm/1 inch lengths	¼ lb green beans, cut into 1 inch lengths
1 onion, finely chopped	1 onion, finely chopped
25 g/1 oz butter	2 tablespoons butter
25 g/1 oz wholemeal flour	¼ cup wholemeal flour
150 ml/¼ pint skimmed milk	⅔ cup skimmed milk
1 teaspoon mild mustard	1 teaspoon mild mustard
Topping	*Topping*
50 g/2 oz Edam cheese, grated	½ cup grated Edam cheese
1 onion, sliced into rings	1 onion, sliced into rings
1 tomato, sliced into rings	1 tomato, sliced into rings
parsley sprigs	parsley sprigs

Cook the potatoes in boiling salted water until tender. Drain, reserving some of the liquid. Mash the potatoes, adding salt and pepper to taste and a little potato liquid if necessary to make the mixture soft enough to pipe. Leave the potato to cool slightly, then spoon into a piping bag with a large plain nozzle attached. Pipe a 20 cm/8 inch flan case (pie shell) shape on an ovenproof plate.

Place the celery, carrots, cauliflower, peas, beans and onion in a pan, cover with lightly salted water and simmer for 5 minutes. Drain the vegetables, reserving 150 ml/¼ pint (⅔ cup) of the vegetable stock.

Melt the butter in a pan and stir in the flour. Gradually stir in the reserved vegetable stock and milk. Bring the sauce to the boil, stirring all the time, until it thickens. Remove from the heat and stir in the vegetables and mustard. Carefully pour into the potato case. Sprinkle the cheese over the top and brown under a preheated moderate grill (broiler) or cook in a preheated moderately hot oven (200°C/400°F, Gas Mark 6) for 20 to 30 minutes.

Garnish with onion and tomato rings and parsley sprigs. Serve immediately.
Serves 4 (approximately 325 calories per portion)

CHEESE SOUFFLÉ TARTLETS

METRIC/IMPERIAL	AMERICAN
Tartlet cases	*Tartlet cases*
25 g/1 oz All Bran cereal	1 cup All Bran cereal
5 tablespoons skimmed milk	$\frac{1}{3}$ cup skimmed milk
50 g/2 oz butter	$\frac{1}{4}$ cup butter
125 g/5 oz plain flour	$1\frac{1}{4}$ cups all-purpose flour
salt	salt
Filling	*Filling*
2 eggs, separated	2 eggs, separated
25 g/1 oz Cheddar cheese, grated	$\frac{1}{4}$ cup grated cheese
pinch of cayenne pepper	pinch of cayenne
1 tablespoon chopped parsley	1 tablespoon chopped parsley

Soak the bran in the milk for 10 minutes.

Rub (cut) the butter into the flour and salt until the mixture resembles breadcrumbs. Add the bran mixture and knead until smooth. Roll out the dough on a lightly floured surface. Using a 6 cm/2½ inch cutter, cut out 12 rounds and place in patty tins (muffin pans); prick the bases well. Cook in a preheated hot oven (220°C/425°F, Gas Mark 7) for 10 minutes.

Beat the egg yolks, cheese, cayenne pepper and parsley together. Whisk the egg whites until stiff and fold into the yolk mixture. Spoon into the cases and cook in the hot oven for a further 10 to 12 minutes. Serve immediately.
Makes 12 (approximately 120 calories each)

GOLDEN FISH FLAN (PIE)

METRIC/IMPERIAL	AMERICAN
Flan case	*Pie shell*
225 g/8 oz plain flour	2 cups all-purpose flour
pinch of salt	pinch of salt
100 g/4 oz low fat spread, frozen hard	$\frac{1}{2}$ cup low fat spread, frozen hard
25 g/1 oz Cheddar cheese, grated	$\frac{1}{4}$ cup grated Cheddar cheese
about 2 tablespoons iced water	about 2 tablespoons iced water
Filling	*Filling*
1 small onion, grated	1 small onion, minced
50 g/2 oz button mushrooms, finely sliced	$\frac{1}{2}$ cup finely sliced button mushrooms
juice of $\frac{1}{2}$ lemon	juice of $\frac{1}{2}$ lemon
225 g/8 oz smoked haddock, cooked and flaked	1 cup cooked and flaked smoked haddock (finnan haddie)
2 eggs	2 eggs
3 tablespoons skimmed milk	3 tablespoons skimmed milk
100 g/4 oz cottage cheese	$\frac{1}{2}$ cup cottage cheese
freshly ground black pepper	freshly ground black pepper
Garnish	*Garnish*
parsley sprigs	parsley sprigs

Sift the flour and salt into a bowl. Grate in the fat. Mix in the cheese and bind together with enough water to make a firm dough. Roll out the dough on a lightly floured surface and line an oval 600 ml/1 pint china ovenproof pie dish. Line with greaseproof (parchment) paper and dried beans and 'bake blind' in a preheated moderately hot oven (190°C/375°F, Gas Mark 5) for 15 minutes. Remove the paper and beans and return to the oven for a further 5 minutes.

Place the onion, mushrooms and lemon juice in a pan and simmer for 5 minutes. Stir in the fish and spread this mixture over the base of the flan. Beat the eggs and milk together, stir in the cheese and pepper to taste. Pour the egg mixture over the fish. Cook in a preheated moderate oven (180°C/350°F, Gas Mark 4) for 30 to 40 minutes until set and golden brown.

Serve hot or cold, garnished with parsley.
Serves 4 (approximately 500 calories per portion)

Golden Fish Flan (Pie); Cheese Soufflé Tartlets

WHOLEMEAL SAVOURY FLAN (PIE)

METRIC/IMPERIAL	AMERICAN
Flan case	*Pie shell*
175 g/6 oz wholemeal flour	1½ cups wholemeal flour
pinch of salt	pinch of salt
75 g/3 oz low fat spread, straight from refrigerator	¼ cup plus 2 tablespoons low fat spread, straight from refrigerator
2 tablespoons iced water	2 tablespoons iced water
Filling	*Filling*
1 green pepper, cored and seeded	1 green pepper, seeded
2 eggs	2 eggs
150 ml/¼ pint skimmed milk	⅔ cup skimmed milk
1 tablespoon tomato purée	1 tablespoon tomato paste
1 onion, grated	1 onion, minced
1 clove garlic, crushed	1 clove garlic, crushed
50 g/2 oz lean ham, chopped	¼ cup chopped lean ham
salt and pepper	salt and pepper
25 g/1 oz Cheddar cheese, grated	¼ cup grated cheese
Garnish	*Garnish*
1 tomato, sliced	1 tomato, sliced
chopped parsley	chopped parsley

Mix the flour and salt together in a mixing bowl. Rub (cut) in the fat until the mixture resembles fine breadcrumbs. Make a well in the centre, add the water and mix to a firm dough. Roll out the dough on a lightly floured surface and line a 20 cm/8 inch flan ring on a baking sheet. Line with greaseproof (parchment) paper and dried beans and 'bake blind' in a preheated moderately hot oven (190°C/375°F, Gas Mark 5) for 10 minutes. Remove paper and beans and return to the oven for 5 minutes.

Slice half the green pepper into rings and reserve; chop the remainder. Whisk together the eggs, milk and tomato purée (paste). Stir in the onion, garlic, chopped pepper, ham and salt and pepper to taste. Pour into the flan case (pie shell). Arrange the pepper rings on top and cover with the cheese. Cook in a preheated moderately hot oven (190°C/375°F, Gas Mark 5) for 25 to 30 minutes. Garnish with sliced tomato and parsley. Serve hot or cold.
Serves 4 (approximately 430 calories per portion)

TOMATO AND ONION FLAN (PIE)

METRIC/IMPERIAL	AMERICAN
Flan case	*Pie shell*
50 g/2 oz low fat spread	¼ cup low fat spread
1 tablespoon iced water	1 tablespoon iced water
100 g/4 oz plain flour	1 cup all-purpose flour
Filling	*Filling*
1 large onion, finely chopped	1 large onion, finely chopped
1 × 425 g/15 oz can tomatoes	1 × 1 lb can tomatoes
1 tablespoon tomato purée	1 tablespoon tomato paste
pinch of dried basil	pinch of dried basil
salt and pepper	salt and pepper
Topping	*Topping*
1 × 50 g/2 oz can anchovy fillets, drained	1 × 2 oz can anchovy fillets, drained
16 black olives	16 ripe olives

Cream together the fat, water and half the flour in a bowl. Gradually work in the remaining flour to make a firm dough. Knead the dough gently on a lightly floured surface. Roll out and line an 18 cm/7 inch plain flan ring on a baking sheet. Line with greaseproof (parchment) paper and dried beans and 'bake blind' in a preheated moderately hot oven (200°C/400°F, Gas Mark 6) for 15 minutes. Remove paper and beans and return to oven for 5 minutes.

Place all the filling ingredients in a pan and cook for about 10 minutes until pulpy, stirring. Pour the filling into the flan case (pie shell).

Top with a lattice of anchovy fillets and olives and cook in a preheated moderate oven (180°C/350°F, Gas Mark 4) for 20 to 30 minutes. Serve warm.
Serves 4 (approximately 220 calories per portion)

CRISPY CHICKEN FLAN (PIE)

METRIC/IMPERIAL	AMERICAN
Flan case	*Pie shell*
15 g/½ oz butter	1 tablespoon butter
2 tablespoons water	2 tablespoons water
2 tablespoons honey	2 tablespoons honey
juice of ½ lemon	juice of ½ lemon
75 g/3 oz puffed rice cereal	3 cups puffed rice cereal
Filling	*Filling*
300 ml/½ pint skimmed milk	1¼ cups skimmed milk
½ onion, chopped	½ onion, chopped
1 bay leaf	1 bay leaf
6 black peppercorns	6 black peppercorns
1 blade mace	1 blade mace
25 g/1 oz butter	2 tablespoons butter
25 g/1 oz plain flour	¼ cup all-purpose flour
1 × 198 g/7 oz can sweetcorn kernels, drained	1 × ½ lb can whole kernel corn, drained
225 g/8 oz cooked chicken, chopped	1 cup chopped cooked chicken
grated rind of 1 lemon	grated rind of 1 lemon
salt and pepper	salt and pepper
Garnish	*Garnish*
finely chopped chives and parsley	finely chopped chives and parsley

To make the flan case (pie shell): place the butter, water, honey and lemon juice in a pan. Bring to the boil and boil for 2 minutes. Pour on to the cereal and mix together. Press the mixture on to the base and up the sides of a greased 20 cm/8 inch plain flan ring on a serving plate. Chill.

Place the milk in a pan with the onion, bay leaf, peppercorns and mace. Bring slowly to the boil. Remove from the heat and leave to stand for 10 minutes. Strain the milk.

Melt the butter in a pan, stir in the flour and cook for 1 minute. Gradually stir in the flavoured milk. Bring the sauce to the boil and stir until it thickens. Remove from the heat. Stir in the corn, chicken, lemon rind and salt and pepper to taste. Leave the mixture to cool, then spoon into the flan case (pie shell) and chill. Remove flan ring and garnish with chopped herbs. Serve cold.
Serves 4 (approximately 400 calories per portion)

Tomato and Onion Flan (Pie); Wholemeal Savoury Flan (Pie)

LEMON CHIFFON FLAN (PIE)

METRIC/IMPERIAL	AMERICAN
Base	*Base*
2 eggs	2 eggs
50 g/2 oz caster sugar	$\frac{1}{4}$ cup sugar
50 g/2 oz wholemeal flour	$\frac{1}{2}$ cup wholemeal flour
finely grated rind of 1 lemon	finely grated rind of 1 lemon
Filling	*Filling*
15 g/$\frac{1}{2}$ oz gelatine	2 envelopes gelatin
75 g/3 oz caster sugar	$\frac{1}{3}$ cup sugar
450 ml/$\frac{3}{4}$ pint hot water	2 cups hot water
juice of 3 lemons	juice of 3 lemons
2 eggs, separated	2 eggs, separated
To decorate	*For decoration*
mimosa balls	mimosa balls
angelica	angelica

To make the base: whisk the eggs and sugar in a heatproof bowl over a pan of hot water until pale and thick enough to leave a trail (this will take about 10 minutes). Lightly fold in the flour and lemon rind. Pour the mixture into a greased and lined 20 cm/8 inch flan tin. Cook in a preheated moderate oven (180°C/350°F, Gas Mark 4) for 15 to 20 minutes until the sponge springs back when lightly pressed. Leave to cool slightly in the tin, then turn out on to a wire rack and peel off the paper.

Dissolve the gelatine and sugar in a pan in 150 ml/$\frac{1}{4}$ pint ($\frac{2}{3}$ cup) of the hot water. Remove from the heat and add the lemon juice. Whisk the egg yolks in a heatproof bowl and gradually whisk in the remaining 300 ml/$\frac{1}{2}$ pint (1$\frac{1}{4}$ cups) hot water. Place the bowl over a pan of hot water and stir the mixture until slightly thickened. Remove from the heat and add to the gelatine mixture. Chill until at setting point.

Whisk the egg whites and carefully fold into the mixture. Pour into flan case and chill until set. Serve cold, decorated with mimosa balls and angelica.

Serves 6 (approximately 200 calories per portion)

MOCHA SWIRL FLAN (PIE)

METRIC/IMPERIAL	AMERICAN
Base	*Base*
3 eggs	3 eggs
75 g/3 oz caster sugar	$\frac{1}{3}$ cup sugar
75 g/3 oz plain flour	$\frac{3}{4}$ cup all-purpose flour
Filling	*Filling*
225 g/8 oz marshmallows	$\frac{1}{2}$ lb marshmallows
25 g/1 oz caster sugar	2 tablespoons sugar
150 ml/$\frac{1}{4}$ pint evaporated milk	$\frac{2}{3}$ cup evaporated milk
2 teaspoons instant coffee powder	2 teaspoons instant coffee powder
1 tablespoon cocoa powder	1 tablespoon unsweetened cocoa
120 ml/4 fl oz whipping cream	$\frac{1}{2}$ cup whipping cream
1 tablespoon skimmed milk	1 tablespoon skimmed milk

Whisk the eggs and sugar in a heatproof bowl over a pan of hot water until thick and pale in colour. Remove from the heat and continue whisking until cool. Lightly fold in the flour. Pour the mixture into a greased and lined 23 cm/9 inch sponge flan tin (Mary Ann pan). Cook immediately in a preheated moderate oven (180°C/350°F, Gas Mark 4) for 20 to 30 minutes. Leave to cool slightly in the tin, then turn out on to a wire rack and peel off the paper.

Reserve 6 marshmallows for decoration. Cut up the remaining marshmallows and place in a pan with the sugar, evaporated milk, coffee and cocoa and stir the mixture over a low heat until smooth. Remove from the heat and leave to cool, stirring occasionally. Whip the cream and gently fold in the marshmallow mixture. Spoon into the sponge cake case.

Cut up the remaining 6 marshmallows, place in a pan with the milk and melt over a low heat. Swirl this mixture into the chocolate filling in the flan. Serve cold.
Serves 8 (approximately 250 calories per portion)

LOGANBERRY MERINGUE FLAN (PIE)

METRIC/IMPERIAL	AMERICAN
Base	*Base*
4 egg whites	4 egg whites
225 g/8 oz icing sugar, sieved	scant 2 cups sifted confectioners' sugar
few drops vanilla essence	few drops vanilla extract
Filling	*Filling*
750 g/1$\frac{1}{2}$ lb loganberries	5 cups loganberries

Place the egg whites and icing (confectioners') sugar in a heatproof bowl over a pan of hot water. Whisk until the mixture is very thick and holds its shape (this will take at least 10 minutes). Add the vanilla to taste.

Spoon the meringue into a piping bag fitted with a 1 cm/$\frac{1}{2}$ inch star nozzle and pipe a 20 cm/8 inch round on a baking sheet lined with non-stick (parchment) paper. Then pipe around the edge to build up the sides. Cook in a cool oven (140°C/275°F, Gas Mark 1) for 50 minutes until set and crisp. Remove from the oven, leave to cool and remove paper. Fill with loganberries just before serving.
Serves 8 (approximately 140 calories per portion)

Loganberry Meringue Flan (Pie)

SATSUMA AND APPLE FLAN (PIE)

METRIC/IMPERIAL	AMERICAN
Base	*Base*
75 g/3 oz low fat spread	$\frac{1}{4}$ cup plus 2 tablespoons low fat spread
1$\frac{1}{2}$–2 tablespoons iced water	1$\frac{1}{2}$–2 tablespoons iced water
175 g/6 oz wholemeal flour	1$\frac{1}{2}$ cups wholemeal flour
Filling and topping	*Filling and topping*
2 satsumas	2 satsumas
450 ml/$\frac{3}{4}$ pint thick apple purée (made with 750 g/1$\frac{3}{4}$ lb cooking apples)	2 cups thick apple purée (made with 750 g/1$\frac{3}{4}$ lb cooking apples)
1 tablespoon honey	1 tablespoon honey

Cream together the fat, water and half the flour in a bowl. Gradually work in the remaining flour to make a firm dough. Knead the dough lightly on a floured surface. Roll out the dough and line a 20 cm/8 inch ovenproof deep plate. Roll out the pastry trimmings and cut into thin strips for the lattice. Decorate the pastry edge of the flan.

Finely grate the rind of the satsumas. Cut the fruit into segments, discarding any pips and membranes.

Mix the satsuma rind into the apple purée and spoon into the flan. Arrange the pastry strips in a lattice design over the top. Mix the satsuma segments with the honey, then arrange on the flan between the lattice. Cook in a preheated moderately hot oven (200°C/400°F, Gas Mark 6) for 25 to 30 minutes. Serve hot or cold.
Serves 6 (approximately 200 calories per portion)

BANANA CUSTARD FLAN (PIE)

METRIC/IMPERIAL	AMERICAN
Flan case	*Pie shell*
75 g/3 oz low fat spread	$\frac{1}{4}$ cup plus 2 tablespoons low fat spread
1$\frac{1}{2}$–2 tablespoons iced water	1$\frac{1}{2}$–2 tablespoons iced water
175 g/6 oz plain flour	1$\frac{1}{2}$ cups all-purpose flour
Filling	*Filling*
1 banana	1 banana
3 eggs	3 eggs
250 ml/8 fl oz skimmed milk	1 cup skimmed milk
1 teaspoon caster sugar	1 teaspoon caster sugar
Topping	*Topping*
1 banana	1 banana
1 tablespoon brown sugar	1 tablespoon brown sugar

Cream together the fat, water and half the flour in a bowl. Gradually work in the remaining flour to make a firm dough. Knead the dough lightly on a floured surface. Roll out the dough and line a 20 cm/8 inch fluted flan ring on a baking sheet. Line with greaseproof (parchment) paper and dried beans and 'bake blind' in a preheated moderately hot oven (200°C/400°F, Gas Mark 6) for 15 minutes. Remove paper and beans and return to the oven for 5 to 10 minutes.

Slice the banana and arrange in the flan case (pie shell). Whisk together the eggs, milk and sugar and strain into the flan over the banana. Cook in a preheated moderate oven (160°C/325°F, Gas Mark 3) for 25 to 30 minutes until the filling is set. Slice the banana on to the set custard and sprinkle over the brown sugar. Place under a preheated grill (broiler) for a few seconds for the sugar to caramelise. Serve immediately.
Serves 6 (approximately 250 calories per portion)

RHUBARB MERINGUE FLAN (PIE)

METRIC/IMPERIAL	AMERICAN
Flan case	*Pie shell*
175 g/6 oz plain flour	1½ cups all-purpose flour
75 g/3 oz low fat spread, straight from refrigerator	¼ cup plus 2 tablespoons low fat spread, straight from refrigerator
2 tablespoons iced water	2 tablespoons iced water
Filling	*Filling*
450 g/1 lb rhubarb	1 lb rhubarb
4 tablespoons water	4 tablespoons water
25 g/1 oz cornflour	¼ cup cornstarch
2 egg yolks	2 egg yolks
1 tablespoon red jam	1 tablespoon red jam
Topping	*Topping*
2 egg whites	2 egg whites
75 g/3 oz caster sugar	⅓ cup sugar

Sift the flour into a mixing bowl and rub (cut) in the fat. Add the water and mix to form a firm dough. Roll out the dough on a lightly floured surface and line a 20 cm/8 inch flan dish. Line with greaseproof (parchment) paper and dried beans and 'bake blind' in a preheated moderately hot oven (190°C/375°F, Gas Mark 5) for 10 to 15 minutes. Remove paper and beans and return to the oven for 5 minutes.

Cut the rhubarb into 2.5 cm/1 inch pieces. Place the rhubarb and 2 tablespoons of the water in a pan and cook over a low heat until tender. Blend the cornflour (cornstarch) with the remaining 2 tablespoons water. Stir into the rhubarb and bring to the boil, stirring all the time. Stir the fruit until thick. Remove the pan from the heat and beat in the egg yolks and jam. Whisk the egg whites until stiff. Whisk in one-third of the sugar, then another third and finally whisk in the remaining sugar.

Spoon the rhubarb into the flan case (pie shell) and pipe the meringue on top. Cook in a cool oven (140°C/275°F, Gas Mark 1) for 1 to 1½ hours until the meringue is dry and tinged golden. Serve cold.
Serves 6 (approximately 230 calories per portion)

BLACKCURRANT CHEESECAKE

METRIC/IMPERIAL	AMERICAN
Base	*Base*
25 g/1 oz low fat spread, melted	2 tablespoons low fat spread, melted
1 tablespoon honey	1 tablespoon honey
50 g/2 oz puffed rice cereal	2 cups puffed rice cereal
Filling	*Filling*
225 g/8 oz blackcurrants	2 cups blackcurrants
120 ml/4 fl oz water	½ cup water
1 packet blackcurrant jelly	1 package blackcurrant-flavored gelatin
5 tablespoons evaporated milk	⅓ cup evaporated milk
225 g/8 oz cottage cheese	1 cup cottage cheese
175 g/6 oz curd cheese	⅔ cup curd cheese
Topping	*Topping*
½ packet blackcurrant jelly	½ package blackcurrant-flavored gelatin
5 tablespoons hot water	⅓ cup hot water
225 g/8 oz blackcurrants	2 cups blackcurrants

Mix the fat, honey and cereal together and press over the bottom of a greased 25 cm/10 inch loose-bottomed cake tin (springform pan). Chill the base.

Cook the blackcurrants in the water until soft. Liquidise and sieve the fruit to make a smooth purée. Heat the purée in a pan, add the blackcurrant jelly (gelatin) and stir until dissolved. Leave to cool. Whip the evaporated milk until thick. Mix the cheeses together with the evaporated milk, then stir in the cool jelly. Pour on to the base and chill until set.

Melt the jelly (gelatin) for the topping in the hot water. Add the blackcurrants and make up to 250 ml/8 fl oz (1 cup) with water if necessary. When just at setting point, spoon on to filling and chill until set. Remove from the tin and serve chilled.
Serves 10 (approximately 180 calories per portion)

JOYFUL CHEESECAKE

METRIC/IMPERIAL	AMERICAN
Base	*Base*
175 g/6 oz digestive biscuits, crushed	1½ cups crushed graham crackers
50 g/2 oz low fat spread, melted	½ cup low fat spread, melted
Filling	*Filling*
450 g/1 lb curd cheese	2 cups curd cheese
2 eggs	2 eggs
50 g/2 oz caster sugar	¼ cup sugar
finely grated rind and juice of 1 lemon	finely grated rind and juice of 1 lemon
few drops of vanilla essence	few drops of vanilla extract
Topping	*Topping*
250 ml/8 fl oz soured cream	1 cup soured cream
40 g/1½ oz caster sugar	3 tablespoons sugar
few drops of vanilla essence	few drops of vanilla extract
1 slice lemon	1 slice lemon

Mix the biscuit (cracker) crumbs with the fat and press over the bottom of a greased 25 cm/10 inch loose-bottomed cake tin (springform pan). Cook in a preheated moderate oven (180°C/350°F, Gas Mark 4) for 5 to 10 minutes. Leave to cool.

Beat the ingredients for the filling together and pour on to the base. Cook in the moderate oven for 30 minutes or until the mixture is shrinking away from the sides. Leave to cool for 15 to 20 minutes.

Mix the topping ingredients together and pour over the filling. Cook in the moderate oven again for a further 10 minutes. Chill. Remove the cheesecake from the tin and decorate with a twisted lemon slice.
Serves 10 (approximately 250 calories per portion)

SUMMER STRAWBERRY CHEESECAKE

METRIC/IMPERIAL
Base
75 g/3 oz sweet biscuits,
  crushed
Filling
15 g/½ oz gelatine
4 tablespoons hot water
225 g/8 oz cottage cheese,
  sieved
1 × 150 g/5 oz carton plain
  yogurt
225 g/8 oz strawberries,
  puréed
2 egg whites
Topping
4 tablespoons double cream,
  whipped
100 g/4 oz strawberries

AMERICAN
Base
¾ cup crushed graham
  crackers
Filling
2 envelopes unflavored
  gelatin
¼ cup hot water
1 cup sieved cottage cheese
⅔ cup plain yogurt
1½ cups strawberries,
  puréed
2 egg whites
Topping
¼ cup heavy cream, whipped
⅔ cup strawberries

Coat the bottom and sides of a lightly greased 20 cm/8 inch loose-bottomed cake tin (springform pan) with the crumbs.

Dissolve the gelatine in the water; leave to cool. Mix the cheese, yogurt and strawberry purée together and stir in the gelatine. Whisk the egg whites until stiff and carefully fold into the strawberry mixture. Pour into the tin (pan) and chill until set.

Carefully remove the cheesecake from the tin. Pipe tiny rosettes of cream on top and decorate with 6 strawberry halves. Slice the remaining strawberries and arrange around the base of cheesecake. Serve cold.

Serves 6 (approximately 150 calories per portion)

Rhubarb Meringue Flan (Pie); Summer Strawberry Cheesecake

MANDARIN CHEESECAKE

METRIC/IMPERIAL	AMERICAN
Base	*Base*
50 g/2 oz rich tea biscuits, crushed	½ cup crushed graham crackers
25 g/1 oz low fat spread, melted	2 tablespoons low fat spread, melted
Filling	*Filling*
15 g/½ oz gelatine	2 envelopes unflavored gelatin
3 tablespoons hot water	3 tablespoons hot water
1 × 300 g/11 oz can mandarin orange segments	1 × 11 oz can mandarin orange segments
225 g/8 oz cottage cheese	1 cup cottage cheese
100 g/4 oz curd cheese	½ cup curd cheese
1 × 150 g/5 oz carton plain yogurt	⅔ cup plain yogurt
25 g/1 oz caster sugar	2 tablespoons sugar
1 egg white	1 egg white
To decorate	*For decoration*
glacé cherries	glacé cherries
angelica	angelica

Mix the biscuit (cracker) crumbs with the melted fat. Press the mixture over the bottom of a greased 18 cm/7 inch loose-bottomed cake tin (springform pan); chill.

Dissolve the gelatine in the hot water. Drain the syrup from the fruit and make up to 150 ml/¼ pint (⅔ cup) with water if necessary. Reserve some mandarin orange segments for decoration and chop the rest.

Place the cheeses, syrup, yogurt and sugar in a liquidiser and blend together. Pour into a large bowl and stir in gelatine and chopped fruit. Whisk the egg white until stiff and carefully fold into mixture. Pour on to the base and chill until set. Remove cheesecake from tin and decorate with reserved mandarin oranges, cherries and angelica. Serve chilled.
Serves 8 (approximately 150 calories per portion)

GINGER AND APPLE CHEESECAKE

METRIC/IMPERIAL	AMERICAN
Base	*Base*
175 g/6 oz plain flour	1½ cups all-purpose flour
1 teaspoon ground ginger	1 teaspoon ground ginger
25 g/1 oz caster sugar	2 tablespoons sugar
75 g/3 oz low fat spread, frozen hard	¼ cup plus 2 tablespoons low fat spread, frozen hard
1 egg yolk	1 egg yolk
1 tablespoon iced water	1 tablespoon iced water
Filling	*Filling*
2 medium dessert apples, quartered, cored and sliced	2 medium-sized apples, quartered, cored and sliced
1 tablespoon lemon juice	1 tablespoon lemon juice
1 tablespoon water	1 tablespoon water
1 egg, separated	1 egg, separated
25 g/1 oz caster sugar	2 tablespoons caster sugar
225 g/8 oz cottage cheese	1 cup cottage cheese
120 ml/4 fl oz soured cream	½ cup soured cream
1 egg white	1 egg white
Topping	*Topping*
1 dessert apple, quartered, cored and thinly sliced	1 apple, quartered, cored and thinly sliced
1 tablespoon clear honey, warmed	1 tablespoon honey, warmed

Mix together the flour, ginger and sugar in a bowl. Grate in the fat and mix in. Bind together with the egg yolk and water. Chill the dough for 30 minutes.

Roll out the dough and line a 20 cm/8 inch fluted flan ring on a baking sheet. Line with greaseproof (parchment) paper and dried beans and 'bake blind' in a preheated moderately hot oven (190°C/375°F, Gas Mark 5) for 10 minutes. Remove paper and beans and return to the oven for 5 minutes.

Gently cook the apples in the lemon juice and water until soft but the slices remain whole. Drain the apple slices, if necessary, and arrange in the flan case (pie shell). Beat the egg yolk and sugar together. Stir in the cheese and cream. Whisk the egg whites until stiff and fold into the cheese mixture. Spoon on to the apples and cook in a preheated moderate oven (180°C/350°F, Gas Mark 4) for 20 to 25 minutes.

Decorate with apple slices and brush over the honey as a glaze. If liked, place under a preheated grill (broiler) for a few seconds. Serve hot or cold.
Serves 8 (approximately 250 calories per portion)

PINEAPPLE CHEESECAKE

METRIC/IMPERIAL	AMERICAN
Base	*Base*
75 g/3 oz low fat spread	$\frac{1}{4}$ cup plus 2 tablespoons low fat spread
1 tablespoon golden syrup	1 tablespoon light corn syrup
175 g/6 oz digestive biscuits, crushed	$1\frac{1}{2}$ cups crushed graham crackers
Filling	*Filling*
1 tablespoon cornflour	1 tablespoon cornstarch
25 g/1 oz caster sugar	2 tablespoons sugar
300 ml/$\frac{1}{2}$ pint skimmed milk	$1\frac{1}{4}$ cups skimmed milk
2 eggs, beaten	2 eggs, beaten
225 g/8 oz cottage cheese, sieved	1 cup sieved cottage cheese
few drops vanilla essence	few drops vanilla extract
Topping	*Topping*
1 × 225 g/8 oz can pineapple rings in natural juice	1 × $\frac{1}{2}$ lb can pineapple rings in natural juice
angelica leaves	angelica leaves
$1\frac{1}{2}$ teaspoons cornflour	$1\frac{1}{2}$ teaspoons cornstarch

Melt the fat and syrup in a pan over a low heat and mix in the biscuit (cracker) crumbs. Press over the bottom and up the sides of a 20 cm/8 inch shallow pie dish. Leave to set.

Blend the cornflour (cornstarch) and sugar to a cream with a little of the milk. Bring the remaining milk to the boil in a pan and pour on to the cornflour (cornstarch), stirring all the time. Rinse out the saucepan. Pour the sauce back into the pan and cook for 1 to 2 minutes, stirring all the time. Remove from the heat and whisk in the eggs. Cook for 1 minute, then leave to cool slightly. Whisk in cottage cheese and vanilla to taste. Pour into the crumb case and chill until set.

Drain the juice from the pineapple and make up to 150 ml/$\frac{1}{4}$ pint ($\frac{2}{3}$ cup) with water if necessary. Decorate cheesecake with pineapple and angelica. Blend cornflour (cornstarch) and juice together in a pan. Bring to the boil, stirring all the time, until the glaze thickens and clears. Leave to cool slightly, then spoon over the pineapple. Serve chilled.
Serves 8 (approximately 220 calories per portion)

Honey and Lemon Cheesecake

HONEY AND LEMON CHEESECAKE

METRIC/IMPERIAL	AMERICAN
Base	*Base*
100 g/4 oz digestive biscuits, crushed	1 cup crushed graham crackers
50 g/2 oz low fat spread, melted	$\frac{1}{4}$ cup low fat spread, melted
finely grated rind of $\frac{1}{2}$ lemon	finely grated rind of $\frac{1}{2}$ lemon
Filling	*Filling*
225 g/8 oz cottage cheese	1 cup cottage cheese
120 ml/4 fl oz plain yogurt	$\frac{1}{2}$ cup plain yogurt
4 tablespoons clear honey	$\frac{1}{4}$ cup honey
2 eggs	2 eggs
squeeze of lemon juice	squeeze of lemon juice
pinch of salt	pinch of salt
$\frac{1}{4}$ teaspoon ground cinnamon	$\frac{1}{4}$ teaspoon ground cinnamon
Topping	*Topping*
18 flaked almonds	18 slivered almonds
icing sugar	confectioners' sugar

Mix the biscuit (cracker) crumbs, fat and lemon rind together and press over the bottom of a greased 20 cm/8 inch loose-bottomed cake tin (springform pan).

Place the cheese, yogurt, honey, eggs, lemon juice and salt into a liquidiser and blend until smooth. Pour on to the base. Sprinkle over the cinnamon. Cook in a preheated moderate oven (160°C/325°F, Gas Mark 3) for 45 minutes. Remove from oven and arrange almonds on top.

When cold, remove cheesecake from tin. Sieve icing (confectioners') sugar over the cheesecake.
Serves 6 (approximately 220 calories per portion)

COOKED SWEET CHEESECAKES

Classic cooked cheesecakes make stylish desserts, and can also be served to accompany tea or coffee.

LEMON CRUMB CHEESECAKE

METRIC/IMPERIAL	AMERICAN
Base	*Base*
50 g/2 oz butter	¼ cup butter
175 g/6 oz fresh breadcrumbs	3 cups soft bread crumbs
50 g/2 oz demerara sugar	¼ cup raw sugar
grated rind of ½ lemon	grated rind of ½ lemon
Filling	*Filling*
3 eggs, separated	3 eggs, separated
100 g/4 oz caster sugar	½ cup sugar
350 g/12 oz curd cheese	1½ cups small curd cottage cheese
150 ml/¼ pint single cream	⅔ cup light cream
grated rind and juice of 1 lemon	grated rind and juice of 1 lemon
Topping	*Topping*
25 g/1 oz chopped nuts	¼ cup chopped nuts
lemon twists	lemon twists

Melt the butter in a pan and add the breadcrumbs. Heat gently, stirring, until lightly browned. Stir in the sugar and lemon rind. Allow to cool. Press two-thirds of the mixture over the bottom of a greased 20 cm/8 inch loose-bottomed cake tin (springform pan).

Beat together the egg yolks and sugar until creamy, then blend in the cheese, cream, lemon rind and juice. Whisk the egg whites until just frothy and fold into the mixture. Pour over the crumb base and cook in a preheated moderate oven (160°C/325°F, Gas Mark 3) for 50 minutes or until cooked. Sprinkle the remaining crumb mixture and nuts over the top of the cheesecake and return to the oven for 15 minutes. Leave to cool in the tin (pan). Remove and place on a serving platter. Decorate with lemon twists and serve chilled with whipped cream.
Serves 8

RICH CONTINENTAL CHEESECAKE

METRIC/IMPERIAL	AMERICAN
Base	*Base*
100 g/4 oz self-raising flour	1 cup self-rising flour
65 g/2½ oz butter	¼ cup plus 1 tablespoon butter
25 g/1 oz icing sugar	¼ cup confectioners' sugar
1 egg yolk	1 egg yolk
Filling	*Filling*
50 g/2 oz butter	¼ cup butter
50 g/2 oz sugar	¼ cup sugar
2 eggs, separated	2 eggs, separated
150 ml/¼ pint double cream	⅔ cup heavy cream
25 g/1 oz ground almonds	¼ cup ground almonds
225 g/8 oz cream cheese	1 cup cream cheese
grated rind and juice of 1 lemon	grated rind and juice of 1 lemon
To decorate	*For decoration*
sifted icing sugar	sifted confectioners' sugar

Sift the flour into a bowl and rub (cut) in the butter until the mixture resembles fine breadcrumbs. Stir in the icing (confectioners') sugar and bind the mixture together with the egg yolk. Chill the dough for 30 minutes. Roll out and line a 23 cm/9 inch flan dish (pie pan).

Cream together the butter and sugar until pale and fluffy, then beat in the egg yolks. Blend in the cream, ground almonds, cream cheese, lemon rind and juice. Beat well. Whisk the egg whites until stiff and fold into the mixture. Pour into the pastry case (pie shell) and cook in a preheated moderate oven (180°C/350°F, Gas Mark 4) for 50 minutes or until cooked. If the top is browning too quickly, lower the oven temperature to 160°C/325°F, Gas Mark 3. Serve warm or chilled dusted with icing (confectioners') sugar.
Serves 6 to 8

SOURED CREAM AND PRUNE CHEESECAKE

METRIC/IMPERIAL	AMERICAN
Base	*Base*
100 g/4 oz plain flour	1 cup all-purpose flour
pinch of salt	pinch of salt
25 g/1 oz margarine	2 tablespoons margarine
25 g/1 oz lard	2 tablespoons shortening
1 tablespoon water	1 tablespoon water
Filling	*Filling*
225 g/8 oz curd cheese	1 cup curd cheese
25 g/1 oz plain flour	$\frac{1}{4}$ cup all-purpose flour
50 g/2 oz soft brown sugar	$\frac{1}{3}$ cup light brown sugar
2 eggs, beaten	2 eggs, beaten
150 ml/$\frac{1}{4}$ pint soured cream	$\frac{2}{3}$ cup sour cream
75 g/3 oz prunes, soaked	$\frac{1}{2}$ cup prunes, soaked
Topping	*Topping*
whipped cream	whipped cream
brown sugar	brown sugar

To make the base: sift the flour and salt into a bowl. Rub (cut) in the margarine and lard (shortening) until the mixture resembles fine breadcrumbs. Mix to a stiff dough with the water. Turn on to a floured surface and knead until smooth. Roll out and line a 20 cm/8 inch flan dish (pie pan).

Beat the curd cheese until smooth, then blend in the flour, sugar, eggs and soured cream.

Remove the stones from the prunes. Reserve three for decoration and chop the remainder. Stir into the cheese mixture, then pour into the pastry case (pie shell). Cook in a preheated moderate oven (180°C/350°F, Gas Mark 4) for 50 minutes to 1 hour or until cooked. Allow to cool.

Decorate with whipped cream and the remaining prunes, then chill. Just before serving, sprinkle with brown sugar. Serves 6

Lemon Crumb Cheesecake; Soured Cream and Prune Cheesecake

GOOSEBERRY CHEESECAKE

METRIC/IMPERIAL	AMERICAN
Base	*Base*
100 g/4 oz self-raising flour	1 cup self-rising flour
pinch of salt	pinch of salt
25 g/1 oz margarine	2 tablespoons margarine
25 g/1 oz lard	2 tablespoons shortening
15 g/½ oz caster sugar	1 tablespoon sugar
1 tablespoon water	1 tablespoon water
Filling	*Filling*
350 g/12 oz gooseberries, topped and tailed	2 cups topped and tailed gooseberries
150 g/5 oz caster sugar	⅔ cup sugar
1 tablespoon water	1 tablespoon water
225 g/8 oz curd cheese	1 cup curd cheese
15 g/½ oz custard powder	2 tablespoons Bird's English dessert mix
1 egg, separated	1 egg, separated
Topping	*Topping*
whipped cream	whipped cream
angelica	angelica

Sift the flour and salt into a bowl. Rub (cut) in the margarine and lard (shortening) until the mixture resembles fine bread-crumbs. Stir in the sugar and mix to a soft dough with the water. Turn on to a floured surface and knead until smooth. Roll out and line a 20 cm/8 inch fluted flan dish (pie pan).

Place the gooseberries in a pan with 75 g/3 oz (⅓ cup) of the sugar and water. Simmer for 15 minutes or until the fruit is tender. Allow to cool and drain off any excess liquid. Spoon the fruit into the bottom of the flan case (pie shell).

Beat together the curd cheese, remaining sugar, custard powder (dessert mix) and the egg yolk. Whisk the egg white until stiff and fold into the mixture. Spoon over the gooseber-ries and cook in a preheated moderately hot oven (190°C/375°F, Gas Mark 5) for 30 to 40 minutes or until cooked. Allow to cool.
Decorate with whipped cream and angelica. Serve chilled.
Serves 6

CRUNCHY CHOCOLATE CHEESECAKE

METRIC/IMPERIAL	AMERICAN
Base	*Base*
75 g/3 oz cornflakes, crushed	3 cups crushed cornflakes
75 g/3 oz plain chocolate, melted	½ cup semi-sweet chocolate pieces, melted
1 tablespoon orange juice	1 tablespoon orange juice
25 g/1 oz butter, melted	2 tablespoons melted butter
Filling	*Filling*
225 g/8 oz curd cheese	1 cup curd cheese
4 tablespoons orange yogurt	4 tablespoons orange yogurt
1 tablespoon sugar	1 tablespoon sugar
2 eggs, separated	2 eggs, separated
Topping	*Topping*
1 × 315 g/11 oz can mandarin orange segments, drained	1 × 11 oz can mandarin orange segments, drained
2 tablespoons apricot jam, sieved	2 tablespoons apricot jam, sieved
whipped cream	whipped cream

Mix together the cornflakes, chocolate, orange juice and butter. Press into the base of a 20 cm/8 inch loose-bottomed cake tin (springform pan). Allow to set.

Meanwhile blend the curd cheese with the yogurt, sugar and egg yolks. Whisk the egg whites until stiff and fold into the mixture. Pour over the base and cook in a preheated moderate oven (180°C/350°F, Gas Mark 4) for 35 to 40 minutes. Allow to cool, then carefully remove from the tin (pan).

Arrange the mandarin oranges on top of the cheesecake. Warm the jam and use to glaze the fruit. Pipe whipped cream around the edge. Serve chilled.
Serves 6

SULTANA LATTICE CHEESECAKE

METRIC/IMPERIAL	AMERICAN
Base	*Base*
175 g/6 oz plain flour	1½ cups all-purpose flour
pinch of salt	pinch of salt
75 g/3 oz margarine	⅓ cup margarine
2 tablespoons water	2 tablespoons water
Filling	*Filling*
50 g/2 oz margarine	¼ cup margarine
50 g/2 oz caster sugar	¼ cup sugar
1 teaspoon cornflour	1 teaspoon cornstarch
1 egg, separated	1 egg, separated
225 g/8 oz curd cheese	1 cup curd cheese
4 tablespoons double cream	4 tablespoons heavy cream
juice of ½ lemon	juice of ½ lemon
50 g/2 oz sultanas	⅓ cup golden raisins
To decorate	*For decoration*
sifted icing sugar	sifted confectioners' sugar

Sift the flour and salt into a bowl. Rub (cut) in the margarine until the mixture resembles fine breadcrumbs. Mix to a stiff dough with the water. Turn on to a floured surface and knead until smooth. Reserve one-third of the dough for the lattice strips. Roll out the remainder and line a 20 cm/8 inch flan tin (pie pan). Line with greaseproof (parchment) paper and dried beans and 'bake blind' in a preheated moderately hot oven (200°C/400°F, Gas Mark 6) for 10 minutes. Remove the paper and beans and cook for a further 5 minutes.

Cream together the margarine and sugar until light and fluffy. Beat in the cornflour (cornstarch) and egg yolk. Blend in the curd cheese, cream and lemon juice. Whisk the egg white until stiff and fold into the mixture with the sultanas (golden raisins). Pour into the cooked flan case (pie shell).

Roll out the remaining pastry (dough) and cut into 1 cm/ ½ inch strips. Arrange in a lattice pattern over the cheesecake. Cook in a preheated moderate oven (160°C/325°F, Gas Mark 3) for 40 to 50 minutes or until cooked. Allow to cool. Dust with icing (confectioners') sugar before serving.
Serves 6

Chocolate Sherry Cheesecake; Sultana Lattice Cheesecake

CHOCOLATE SHERRY CHEESECAKE

METRIC/IMPERIAL	AMERICAN
Base	*Base*
175 g/6 oz digestive biscuits, crushed	1½ cups crushed graham crackers
75 g/3 oz margarine, melted	⅓ cup melted margarine
Filling	*Filling*
250 g/9 oz cream cheese	1 cup plus 1 tablespoon cream cheese
2 eggs, beaten	2 eggs, beaten
25 g/1 oz caster sugar	2 tablespoons sugar
1 tablespoon sherry	1 tablespoon sherry
175 g/6 oz plain chocolate, broken into pieces	6 squares (1 oz each) semi-sweet chocolate
Topping	*Topping*
150 ml/¼ pint double cream	⅔ cup heavy cream
grated chocolate	grated chocolate

Mix the biscuit (cracker) crumbs with the margarine and press into the base and up the sides of a 20 cm/8 inch flan dish (pie pan). Allow to cool and set.

Place the cheese in a bowl and soften with a wooden spoon. Blend in the eggs, sugar and sherry, then mix well.

Place the chocolate in a heatproof bowl over a pan of gently simmering water (or in a double boiler) and stir until melted. Beat into the cheese mixture and pour into the flan case (pie shell). Cook in a preheated moderately hot oven (190°C/375°F, Gas Mark 5) for 30 minutes. Allow to cool.

Whip the cream until thick and pipe whirls on top of the cheesecake. Sprinkle with grated chocolate. Serve chilled.
Serves 6

COCONUT CINNAMON CHEESECAKE

METRIC/IMPERIAL	AMERICAN
Base	*Base*
50 g/2 oz butter	$\frac{1}{4}$ cup butter
50 g/2 oz caster sugar	$\frac{1}{4}$ cup sugar
40 g/1$\frac{1}{2}$ oz plain flour	$\frac{1}{3}$ cup all-purpose flour
75 g/3 oz desiccated coconut	1 cup shredded coconut
Filling	*Filling*
2 eggs, separated	2 eggs, separated
50 g/2 oz soft brown sugar	$\frac{1}{3}$ cup firmly packed light brown sugar
1 teaspoon ground cinnamon	1 teaspoon ground cinnamon
25 g/1 oz cornflour	$\frac{1}{4}$ cup cornstarch
200 ml/$\frac{1}{3}$ pint milk	$\frac{7}{8}$ cup milk
225 g/8 oz cottage cheese, sieved	1 cup sieved cottage cheese
Topping	*Topping*
150 ml/$\frac{1}{4}$ pint double cream	$\frac{2}{3}$ cup heavy cream
25 g/1 oz desiccated coconut, toasted	$\frac{1}{3}$ cup toasted shredded coconut

Cream together the butter and sugar until light and fluffy. Mix in the flour and coconut. Press the mixture in to the base and up the sides of a 23 cm/9 inch flan dish (pie pan). Chill for 30 minutes. Cook in a preheated moderate oven (180°C/350°F, Gas Mark 4) for 20 minutes until golden. Leave to cool.

Beat together the egg yolks, brown sugar and cinnamon. Blend the cornflour (cornstarch) with a little of the cold milk. Heat the remainder until almost boiling then pour on to the cornflour (cornstarch) mixture, stirring continuously. Return to the pan with the egg mixture and heat, stirring, until the mixture thickens. Cool slightly, then fold in the cottage cheese. Whisk the egg whites until stiff and fold into the mixture. Spoon into the flan case (pie shell) and chill.

Whip the cream until thick and pipe a lattice pattern over the top of the cheesecake. Sprinkle with toasted coconut. Serve chilled.

Serves 8

Note: this is a soft cheesecake and will not set firmly.

CHOCOLATE SPICE CHEESECAKE

METRIC/IMPERIAL	AMERICAN
Base	*Base*
100 g/4 oz chocolate digestive biscuits, crushed	1 cup chocolate graham cracker crumbs
40 g/1½ oz margarine, melted	3 tablespoons melted margarine
½ teaspoon ground cinnamon	½ teaspoon ground cinnamon
½ teaspoon grated nutmeg	½ teaspoon grated nutmeg
Filling	*Filling*
2 eggs	2 eggs
50 g/2 oz caster sugar	¼ cup sugar
225 g/8 oz curd cheese	1 cup curd cheese
25 g/1 oz plain flour	¼ cup all-purpose flour
100 g/4 oz plain chocolate, melted	⅔ cup melted semi-sweet chocolate
4 tablespoons double cream	4 tablespoons heavy cream
Topping	*Topping*
chocolate curls	chocolate curls
grated nutmeg	grated nutmeg

Mix together the biscuit (cracker) crumbs, margarine, cinnamon and nutmeg and press over the bottom of a 20 cm/8 inch loose-bottomed cake tin (springform pan).

Whisk together the eggs and sugar until thick. Place the curd cheese in a bowl and blend in the flour, chocolate and cream. Gradually add the egg mixture and beat thoroughly. Pour on to the base and cook in a preheated moderate oven (180°C/350°F, Gas Mark 4) for 45 minutes until cooked. Allow to cool.

Decorate with chocolate curls and grated nutmeg. Serve chilled.

Serves 6

RHUBARB AND GINGER CHEESECAKE

METRIC/IMPERIAL	AMERICAN
Base	*Base*
100 g/4 oz digestive biscuits, crushed	1 cup crushed graham crackers
50 g/2 oz margarine, melted	¼ cup melted margarine
½ teaspoon ground ginger	½ teaspoon ground ginger
Filling	*Filling*
225 g/8 oz rhubarb, chopped	2 cups chopped rhubarb
2 pieces stem ginger, chopped	2 pieces preserved ginger, chopped
25 g/1 oz granulated sugar	2 tablespoons sugar
1 tablespoon ginger syrup	1 tablespoon ginger syrup
225 g/8 oz cream cheese	1 cup cream cheese
150 ml/¼ pint plain yogurt	⅔ cup plain yogurt
2 eggs, separated	2 eggs, separated
50 g/2 oz soft brown sugar	¼ cup light brown sugar
25 g/1 oz plain flour	¼ cup all-purpose flour
Topping	*Topping*
150 ml/¼ pint soured cream	⅔ cup sour cream
25 g/1 oz caster sugar	2 tablespoons sugar
stem ginger	preserved ginger
whipped cream	whipped cream

Mix together the biscuit (cracker) crumbs, margarine and ginger. Press the mixture over the bottom of a 20 cm/8 inch loose-bottomed cake tin (springform pan).

Place the rhubarb, ginger, white sugar and syrup in a pan and cook gently until the fruit is just tender. Cool and spoon over the base.

Blend together the cheese, yogurt, egg yolks, brown sugar and flour and beat well together. Whisk the egg whites until stiff and fold into the cheese mixture. Pour over the rhubarb and cook in a preheated moderate oven (180°C/350°F, Gas Mark 4) for 50 minutes to 1 hour or until firm and beginning to brown. Mix the soured cream with the sugar and spread over the cheesecake. Return to the oven for 10 minutes. Allow to cool, then remove the cheesecake from the tin (pan). Decorate with the ginger and pipe whirls of cream on top. Serve chilled.

Serves 6 to 8

GRAPEFRUIT AND HONEY CHEESECAKE

METRIC/IMPERIAL	AMERICAN
Base	*Base*
100 g/4 oz plain flour	1 cup all-purpose flour
pinch of salt	pinch of salt
25 g/1 oz margarine	2 tablespoons margarine
25 g/1 oz lard	2 tablespoons shortening
1 tablespoon water	1 tablespoon water
Filling	*Filling*
350 g/12 oz cream cheese	1½ cups cream cheese
1 tablespoon clear honey	1 tablespoon honey
50 g/2 oz caster sugar	¼ cup sugar
2 eggs, beaten	2 eggs, beaten
½ × small can frozen concentrated grapefruit juice, thawed	½ × small can frozen concentrated grapefruit juice, thawed
Topping	*Topping*
2 grapefruit	2 grapefruit
2 tablespoons clear honey	2 tablespoons honey
1 tablespoon water	1 tablespoon water
demerara sugar	raw sugar

Sift the flour and salt into a bowl and rub (cut) in the margarine and lard (shortening) until the mixture resembles fine breadcrumbs. Mix to a stiff dough with the water. Turn on to a floured surface and knead until smooth. Roll out and line a 20 cm/8 inch flan dish (pie pan). Line with greaseproof (parchment) paper and dried beans and 'bake blind' in a preheated moderately hot oven (190°C/375°F, Gas Mark 5) for 10 minutes. Remove the paper and beans and cook for a further 5 minutes. Allow to cool.

Place the cream cheese in a bowl and blend in the honey and sugar. Gradually beat in the eggs, then stir in the grapefruit juice. Pour into the pastry case (pie shell) and cook in a preheated moderate oven (160°C/325°F, Gas Mark 3) for 30 to 40 minutes or until cooked. Allow to cool.

Peel the grapefruit, discarding all white pith, and cut into segments. Arrange the grapefruit on top of the cheesecake. Place the honey and water in a pan and heat gently. Use to glaze the fruit. Chill for several hours. Before serving sprinkle with demerara (raw) sugar.

Serves 6 to 8

Grapefruit and Honey Cheesecake; Coconut Cinnamon Cheesecake

PINEAPPLE AND CHERRY CHEESECAKE

METRIC/IMPERIAL	AMERICAN
Base	*Base*
100 g/4 oz digestive biscuits, crushed	1 cup crushed graham crackers
50 g/2 oz butter, melted	¼ cup melted butter
finely grated rind of 1 lemon	finely grated rind of 1 lemon
Filling	*Filling*
225 g/8 oz cottage cheese, sieved	1 cup sieved cottage cheese
2 eggs, beaten	2 eggs, beaten
50 g/2 oz caster sugar	¼ cup sugar
juice of ½ lemon	juice of ½ lemon
Topping	*Topping*
150 ml/¼ pint soured cream	⅔ cup sour cream
fresh or canned pineapple rings	fresh or canned pineapple rings
fresh cherries, stoned and halved	fresh cherries, pitted and halved

Mix together the biscuit (cracker) crumbs, butter and lemon rind. Press into an 18 cm/7 inch flan ring on a baking sheet. Allow to cool and harden.

Mix the cottage cheese with the eggs, sugar and lemon juice. Pour on to the base and cook in a preheated moderately hot oven (190°C/375°F, Gas Mark 5) for 20 minutes or until firm. Remove the cheesecake from the oven and spread the soured cream over the top. Return to the oven for 5 to 10 minutes. Leave to cool. Carefully remove the ring and place the cheesecake on a serving plate. Decorate with the pineapple and cherries. Serve chilled.
Serves 6

CHRISTMAS FRUIT CHEESECAKE

METRIC/IMPERIAL	AMERICAN
Base	*Base*
75 g/3 oz digestive biscuits, crushed	¾ cup crushed graham crackers
Filling	*Filling*
150 g/5 oz butter	½ cup plus 2 tablespoons butter
150 g/5 oz curd cheese	½ cup plus 2 tablespoons curd cheese
150 g/5 oz caster sugar	⅔ cup sugar
65 g/2½ oz ground almonds	½ cup ground almonds
65 g/2½ oz plain flour	½ cup all-purpose flour
5 eggs, separated	5 eggs, separated
2 tablespoons rum	2 tablespoons rum
50 g/2 oz raisins	⅓ cup raisins
50 g/2 oz currants	⅓ cup currants
50 g/2 oz dates, chopped	⅓ cup chopped dates
Topping	*Topping*
150 ml/¼ pint double cream	⅔ cup heavy cream
25 g/1 oz flaked almonds, toasted	¼ cup slivered almonds, toasted
6 dates, stoned and halved	6 dates, stoned and halved

Sprinkle the biscuit (cracker) crumbs over the bottom of a greased 20 cm/8 inch loose-bottomed cake tin (springform pan).

Cream together the butter and cream cheese. Blend in the sugar, ground almonds, flour, egg yolks and rum. Beat well, then stir in the raisins, currants and dates. Whisk the egg whites until stiff and fold into the mixture. Spoon over the base and cook in a preheated moderately hot oven (200°C/400°F, Gas Mark 6) for 15 minutes. Reduce the temperature to moderate (180°C/350°F, Gas Mark 4). Continue to cook the cheesecake for a further 35 to 45 minutes or until golden and firm. Leave to cool, then carefully remove from the tin (pan).

Whip the cream until thick and spread half over the top of the cheesecake. Pipe the remaining cream around the edge. Decorate with the almonds and dates. Serve chilled.
Serves 8 to 10

Christmas Fruit Cheesecake; Red Fruit Cheesecake

RED FRUIT CHEESECAKE

METRIC/IMPERIAL	AMERICAN
Base	*Base*
175 g/6 oz shortcake biscuits, crushed	1½ cups crushed shortcake cookies
75 g/3 oz butter, melted	⅓ cup melted butter
Filling	*Filling*
450 g/1 lb cottage cheese, sieved	2 cups sieved cottage cheese
150 ml/¼ pint milk	⅔ cup milk
2 eggs, separated	2 eggs, separated
50 g/2 oz cornflour	½ cup cornstarch
150 g/5 oz caster sugar	⅔ cup sugar
1 teaspoon vanilla essence	1 teaspoon vanilla extract
Topping	*Topping*
150 ml/¼ pint double cream	⅔ cup heavy cream
fresh raspberries, strawberries, redcurrants, cherries	fresh raspberries, strawberries, red currants, cherries

Mix together the biscuit (cookie) crumbs and butter and press over the bottom of a 20 cm/8 inch loose-bottomed cake tin (springform pan).

Place the cottage cheese in a bowl and blend in the milk, egg yolks, cornflour (cornstarch), sugar and vanilla. Whisk the egg whites until stiff and fold into the cheese mixture. Pour on to the base and cook in a preheated moderate oven (180°C/350°F, Gas Mark 4) for 30 to 40 minutes or until cooked. Leave to cool before removing the cheesecake from the tin (pan).

Whip the cream until thick. Spread half the cream over the top of the cheesecake and pipe the remainder around the edge. Arrange a selection of washed and prepared red fruits in the centre. Serve chilled.
Serves 8 to 10

PINEAPPLE AND WALNUT CHEESECAKE

METRIC/IMPERIAL	AMERICAN
Base	*Base*
100 g/4 oz digestive biscuits, crushed	1 cup graham cracker crumbs
50 g/2 oz butter, melted	$\frac{1}{4}$ cup melted butter
25 g/1 oz sugar	2 tablespoons sugar
50 g/2 oz walnuts, chopped	$\frac{1}{2}$ cup chopped walnuts
Filling	*Filling*
1 × 425 g/15 oz can pineapple rings	1 × 15 oz can pineapple rings
225 g/8 oz cream cheese	1 cup cream cheese
50 g/2 oz caster sugar	$\frac{1}{4}$ cup sugar
25 g/1 oz plain flour	$\frac{1}{4}$ cup all-purpose flour
2 eggs, separated	2 eggs, separated
Topping	*Topping*
150 ml/$\frac{1}{4}$ pint double cream	$\frac{2}{3}$ cup heavy cream
walnut halves	walnut halves

Mix together the biscuit (cracker) crumbs, butter, sugar and walnuts. Press over the bottom of a 20 cm/8 inch loose-bottomed cake tin (springform pan).

Drain the pineapple rings and reserve 1 tablespoon syrup. Blend this syrup with the cheese, then gradually mix in the sugar, flour and egg yolks. Reserve 3 pineapple rings for decoration and chop the remainder. Whisk the egg whites until stiff and fold into the cheese mixture with the chopped pineapple. Pour over the base and cook in a preheated moderate oven (180°C/350°F, Gas Mark 4) for 45 minutes or until cooked. Leave to cool, then remove from the tin (pan).

Whip the cream until thick then use to decorate the cheesecake with the reserved pineapple and walnuts. Serve chilled.

Serves 6 to 8

VELVET MINT CHEESECAKE

METRIC/IMPERIAL	AMERICAN
Base	*Base*
100 g/4 oz self-raising flour	1 cup self-rising flour
65 g/2$\frac{1}{2}$ oz butter	$\frac{1}{4}$ cup plus 1 tablespoon butter
25 g/1 oz icing sugar, sifted	$\frac{1}{4}$ cup sifted confectioners' sugar
1 egg yolk	1 egg yolk
Filling	*Filling*
225 g/8 oz cottage cheese, sieved	1 cup sieved cottage cheese
100 g/4 oz cream cheese	$\frac{1}{2}$ cup cream cheese
50 g/2 oz caster sugar	$\frac{1}{4}$ cup sugar
2 eggs, separated	2 eggs, separated
1 teaspoon peppermint essence	1 teaspoon peppermint extract
$\frac{1}{2}$ teaspoon vanilla essence	$\frac{1}{2}$ teaspoon vanilla
Topping	*Topping*
whipped cream	whipped cream
chocolate mints	chocolate mints

Sift the flour into a bowl. Rub (cut) in the butter until the mixture resembles fine breadcrumbs. Stir in the icing (confectioners') sugar, then bind together with the egg yolk. Chill for 30 minutes. Roll out and line a 20 cm/8 inch flan dish (pie pan).

Blend the cheeses together, then gradually beat in the sugar, egg yolks, peppermint and vanilla. Whisk the egg whites until stiff and fold into the mixture. Pour into the flan case (pie shell) and cook in a preheated moderate oven (180°C/350°F, Gas Mark 4) for 40 to 45 minutes or until cooked. Leave to cool.

Decorate the cheesecake with whipped cream and chocolate mints. Serve chilled.

Serves 6 to 8

BAKED BLACKCURRANT CHEESECAKE

METRIC/IMPERIAL	AMERICAN
Base	*Base*
75 g/3 oz digestive biscuits, crushed	¾ cup crushed graham crackers
40 g/1½ oz margarine, melted	3 tablespoons melted margarine
Filling	*Filling*
225 g/8 oz cream cheese	1 cup cream cheese
50 g/2 oz caster sugar	¼ cup sugar
2 eggs, separated	2 eggs, separated
4 tablespoons blackcurrant yogurt	4 tablespoons blackcurrant yogurt
50 g/2 oz ground almonds	½ cup ground almonds
Topping	*Topping*
1 × 425 g/15 oz can blackcurrant pie filling	1 × 15 oz can blackcurrant pie filling

Mix together the biscuit (cracker) crumbs and margarine, then press over the bottom of a 20 cm/8 inch loose-bottomed cake tin (springform pan).

Place the cheese in a bowl and soften with a wooden spoon. Blend in the sugar, egg yolks, yogurt and ground almonds. Whisk the egg whites until stiff and fold into the mixture. Pour on to the base and cook in a preheated moderate oven (180°C/350°F, Gas Mark 4) for 50 minutes to 1 hour or until cooked. Leave to cool, then remove from the tin (pan).

Cover the top of the cheesecake with the blackcurrant pie filling. Serve chilled.
Serves 6 to 8

SHORTBREAD CHERRY CHEESECAKE

METRIC/IMPERIAL	AMERICAN
Base	*Base*
75 g/3 oz plain flour	¾ cup all-purpose flour
25 g/1 oz caster sugar	2 tablespoons sugar
50 g/2 oz butter	¼ cup butter
Filling	*Filling*
175 g/6 oz cottage cheese, sieved	¾ cup sieved cottage cheese
40 g/1½ oz sugar	3 tablespoons sugar
25 g/1 oz cornflour	¼ cup cornstarch
2 eggs, beaten	2 eggs, beaten
1 tablespoon cherry brandy (optional)	1 tablespoon cherry brandy (optional)
4 tablespoons double cream	4 tablespoons heavy cream
Topping	*Topping*
175 g/6 oz cherry jam	½ cup cherry jam
whipped cream	whipped cream

Sift the flour into a bowl and add the sugar. Rub (cut) in the butter until the mixture resembles fine breadcrumbs. Knead the mixture together. Roll out the shortbread and line the base of a 20 cm/8 inch shallow tin (pan).

Blend together the cottage cheese, sugar, cornflour (cornstarch), eggs, brandy, if used, and cream. Beat well and pour the mixture over the shortbread. Cook in a preheated moderately hot oven (200°C/400°F, Gas Mark 6) for 20 to 30 minutes or until firm. Leave to cool, then remove from the tin (pan).

Spread the jam over the top of the cheesecake and pipe whirls of cream around the edge. Serve chilled.
Serves 6

Velvet Mint Cheesecake; Pineapple and Walnut Cheesecake

UNCOOKED FRUIT CHEESECAKES

The fresh tartness of fruit complements the bland creaminess of gelatine-based cheesecakes. The fruits range from storecupboard stand-bys like tinned pineapple, to exotics such as kiwi fruit.

STRAWBERRY CHEESECAKE

METRIC/IMPERIAL	AMERICAN
100 g/4 oz shortbread biscuits, crushed	1 cup crushed shortbread cookies
40 g/1½ oz butter, melted	3 tablespoons melted butter
225 g/8 oz strawberries	½ lb strawberries
grated rind and juice of ½ orange	grated rind and juice of ½ orange
1 tablespoon gelatine	1 tablespoon unflavored gelatin
3 tablespoons water	3 tablespoons water
175 g/6 oz curd cheese	¾ cup curd cheese
75 g/3 oz caster sugar	6 tablespoons sugar
150 ml/¼ pint double cream	¾ cup heavy cream
1 egg white	1 egg white
To decorate	*For decoration*
8 strawberries	8 strawberries

Mix together the biscuit (cookie) crumbs and butter and press over the bottom of a greased 18 cm/7 inch loose-bottomed cake tin (springform pan). Chill while preparing filling.

Crush the strawberries with the orange rind and juice. Put the gelatine and water into a small heatproof bowl over a pan of hot water and stir until dissolved. Beat together the cheese and sugar. Combine the strawberries and gelatine, then stir into the cheese mixture. Leave to cool.

Whip the cream. Whisk the egg white until stiff. Fold the cream and egg white into the strawberry mixture. Pour into the prepared pan and chill for several hours until set. Remove from the pan and decorate with halved strawberries.
Serves 8

FROZEN APRICOT CHEESECAKE

METRIC/IMPERIAL	AMERICAN
350 g/12 oz dried apricots	2 cups dried apricots
175 g/6 oz caster sugar	¾ cup sugar
150 ml/¼ pint water	⅔ cup water
225 g/8 oz cream cheese	1 cup cream cheese
2 tablespoons medium sherry	2 tablespoons medium sherry
150 ml/¼ pint double cream	⅔ cup heavy cream
about 15 Nice finger biscuits	about 15 plain sweet finger cookies
Topping	*Topping*
fresh or canned apricots	fresh or canned apricots
angelica	angelica

Put the apricots, 50 g/2 oz (¼ cup) of the sugar and the water in a saucepan and simmer for about 30 minutes, stirring occasionally until soft and pulpy. Add the remaining sugar and leave to cool.

Beat the cream cheese and sherry into the apricots. Whip the cream until thick, then fold in. Spoon the apricot mixture into a lightly greased and lined 19 cm/7½ inch shallow square tin (baking pan) and level the surface. Press the biscuits (cookies) on top, cutting where necessary to make them fit. Cover and freeze until required.

Remove the frozen cheesecake from the tin and decorate with apricots and angelica.
Serves 6 to 8

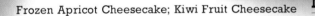

Frozen Apricot Cheesecake; Kiwi Fruit Cheesecake

BLACK FOREST CHEESECAKE

KIWI FRUIT CHEESECAKE

METRIC/IMPERIAL	AMERICAN
4 kiwi fruits	4 kiwi fruits
75 g/3 oz desiccated coconut, toasted	1 cup shredded coconut, toasted
115 g/4½ oz caster sugar	½ cup plus 1 tablespoon sugar
25 g/1 oz butter, melted	2 tablespoons melted butter
225 g/8 oz cream cheese	1 cup cream cheese
4 teaspoons gelatine	4 teaspoons unflavored gelatin
120 ml/4 fl oz sweet white wine	½ cup sweet white wine
250 ml/8 fl oz double cream	1 cup heavy cream
2 egg whites	2 egg whites

Peel and chop two of the kiwi fruits and peel and slice the remaining two.

Mix the coconut, 1 tablespoon of the sugar and the butter together and press over the bottom of a greased 20 cm/8 inch loose-bottomed cake tin (springform pan). Chill the base while preparing filling.

Beat the cheese and remaining sugar together until creamy. Put the gelatine and wine into a small heatproof bowl over a pan of hot water and stir until the gelatine has dissolved. Leave to cool slightly then gradually add to the cheese mixture. Whip the cream until stiff. Whisk the egg whites until stiff. Fold the cream and egg whites into the cheese mixture. Fold in the chopped kiwi fruit. Spoon the mixture into the prepared pan and chill until set. Carefully remove the cheesecake from the pan and decorate with the sliced kiwi fruit.
Serves 8

METRIC/IMPERIAL	AMERICAN
175 g/6 oz bourbon biscuits, crushed	1½ cups crushed chocolate-filled cookies
50 g/2 oz butter, melted	¼ cup butter, melted
1 × 425 g/15 oz can red cherries, stoned	1 × 1 lb can red cherries, pitted
3 tablespoons kirsch	3 tablespoons kirsch
2 tablespoons gelatine	2 tablespoons unflavored gelatin
few drops of red food colouring	few drops of red food coloring
4 tablespoons water	4 tablespoons water
100 g/4 oz plain chocolate	4 squares (1 oz each) semisweet chocolate
100 g/4 oz caster sugar	½ cup sugar
450 g/1 lb cream cheese	2 cups cream cheese
Topping	*Topping*
300 ml/½ pint double cream, whipped	1½ cups heavy cream, whipped
chocolate curls	chocolate curls
cocktail cherries	maraschino cherries

Mix together the biscuit (cookie) crumbs and butter and press over the bottom of a greased 23 cm/9 inch loose-bottomed cake tin (springform pan). Chill while preparing filling.

Drain the cherries and place the syrup in a saucepan. Add 1 tablespoon kirsch and 1 tablespoon gelatine. Place over a gentle heat and stir until the gelatine has dissolved. Add the cherries and a few drops of red food colouring. Chill until on the point of setting. Spoon over the base and chill until set.

Dissolve the remaining gelatine in the water over a gentle heat. Add the remaining kirsch and chocolate and stir until dissolved. Stir in the sugar and cream cheese, cool slightly then spoon over the cherries. Chill until set. Remove from the pan and decorate with cream, chocolate curls and cherries.
Serves 8 to 10

FLORIDA CITRUS CHEESECAKE

METRIC/IMPERIAL	AMERICAN
Base	*Base*
100 g/4 oz digestive biscuits, crushed	1 cup crushed graham crackers
50 g/2 oz margarine, melted	¼ cup margarine, melted
Filling	*Filling*
2 tablespoons gelatine	2 tablespoons unflavored gelatin
175 ml/6 fl oz concentrated frozen grapefruit juice	¾ cup concentrated frozen grapefruit juice
100 g/4 oz light brown sugar	⅔ cup light brown sugar
350 g/12 oz cottage cheese	1½ cups cottage cheese
200 ml/⅓ pint low fat milk	⅞ cup low fat milk
2 egg whites	2 egg whites
Topping	*Topping*
1 grapefruit, peeled and cut into segments	1 grapefruit, peeled and cut into segments
2 oranges, peeled and cut into segments	2 oranges, peeled and cut into segments

Mix together the biscuit (cracker) crumbs and margarine. Press over the base of a greased 20 cm/8 inch loose-bottomed cake tin (springform pan). Chill the base while preparing filling.

Put the gelatine and grapefruit juice into a small heatproof bowl over a pan of hot water and stir until the gelatine has dissolved. Stir in the sugar and leave to cool. Mix the cheese and milk in a blender until smooth. Stir in the gelatine. Chill until just on the point of setting.

Stiffly whisk the egg whites and fold into the chilled mixture. Spoon into the prepared pan and chill until set. Remove the cheesecake from the pan and decorate with grapefruit and orange segments.
Serves 6

Florida Citrus Cheesecake; Russian Cheesecake

RASPBERRY AND STRAWBERRY CHEESECAKE PIE

METRIC/IMPERIAL	AMERICAN
Base	*Base*
350 g/12 oz digestive biscuits, crushed	3 cups crushed graham crackers
175 g/6 oz butter, melted	¾ cup butter, melted
Filling	*Filling*
2 tablets of strawberry jelly	2 tablets strawberry-flavored gelatin
4 tablespoons water	4 tablespoons water
3 eggs, separated	3 eggs, separated
150 ml/¼ pint milk	⅔ cup milk
6 tablespoons lemon juice	6 tablespoons lemon juice
450 g/1 lb cottage cheese	2 cups cottage cheese
25 g/1 oz caster sugar	2 tablespoons sugar
150 ml/¼ pint double cream, whipped	⅔ cup heavy cream
225 g/8 oz raspberries	1⅔ cups raspberries
Topping	*Topping*
whipped cream	whipped cream
raspberries and strawberries	raspberries and strawberries

Mix together the biscuit (cracker) crumbs and butter. Press into the base and up the sides of a 1.8 litre/3 pint china flan dish. Chill the base while preparing filling.

Put the jelly (gelatin) and water in a pan and dissolve over a low heat. Beat together the egg yolks and milk. Stir into the jelly (gelatin) and heat for a few minutes, stirring all the time. Off the heat, add the lemon juice then leave to cool.

Blend the jelly (gelatin) mixture and cheese in a blender until smooth. Whisk the egg whites until stiff, add the sugar and whisk again until stiff. Fold in the cheese mixture, then the cream. Spoon half the mixture into crumb case, cover with the raspberries, then the rest of the mixture. Chill until set. Pipe whirls of cream on top and decorate with raspberries and strawberries.
Serves 8 to 10

BRANDY AND GINGER CHEESECAKE

METRIC/IMPERIAL	AMERICAN
2 tablespoons gelatine	2 tablespoons unflavored gelatin
6 tablespoons water	6 tablespoons water
2 eggs, separated	2 eggs, separated
250 ml/8 fl oz milk	1 cup milk
150 g/5 oz caster sugar	⅔ cup sugar
450 g/1 lb cottage cheese	2 cups cottage cheese
4 tablespoons brandy	4 tablespoons brandy
grated rind and juice of 1 lemon	grated rind and juice of 1 lemon
150 ml/¼ pint double cream	⅔ cup heavy cream
100 g/4 oz stem ginger, chopped	½ cup preserved ginger, chopped
200 g/7 oz gingernut biscuits, crushed	1¾ cups crushed ginger cookies
100 g/4 oz butter, melted	½ cup butter, melted
Topping	*Topping*
whipped cream	whipped cream
chopped stem ginger	chopped preserved ginger
toasted flaked almonds	toasted flaked almonds

Put the gelatine and water into a small heatproof bowl over a pan of hot water and stir until the gelatine has dissolved. Mix together the egg yolks, milk and sugar and place in a heatproof bowl over hot water, stirring occasionally until thickened. Stir in the gelatine.

In a blender, combine the cheese, brandy, lemon rind and juice until smooth. Stir in the egg mixture and chill until just setting. Whip the cream until just thick. Whisk the egg whites until stiff and fold the cream and egg whites into mixture. Stir in the chopped ginger. Pour into a greased and lined 20 cm/8½ inch cake tin (springform pan). Chill until firm.

Mix the biscuit (cookie) crumbs and butter and press gently on top of the cheesecake. Chill until firm.

Invert the cheesecake on to a plate and remove pan. Decorate with swirls of cream, chopped ginger and almonds.
Serves 8 to 10

RUSSIAN CHEESECAKE

METRIC/IMPERIAL
225 g/8 oz cream cheese
50 g/2 oz unsalted butter
150 ml/¼ pint soured cream
2 tablespoons sugar
25 g/1 oz flaked almonds,
   toasted
25 g/1 oz glacé cherries,
   chopped
50 g/2 oz chopped mixed
   peel
50 g/2 oz raisins
8 sponge fingers
To decorate
glacé cherries
angelica

AMERICAN
1 cup cream cheese
¼ cup unsalted butter
⅔ cup sour cream
2 tablespoons sugar
¼ cup flaked almonds, toasted
1½ tablespoons glacé
   cherries, chopped
⅓ cup candied mixed peel
⅓ cup raisins
8 lady fingers
For decoration
glacé cherries
angelica

Beat together the cheese and butter until smooth. Mix in the cream, sugar, almonds, cherries, peel and raisins. Line a 450 g/1 lb loaf tin (pan) with muslin (cheesecloth). Press the cheese mixture into the tin. Press the sponge (lady) fingers on top. Place the tin upside down on a wire tray over a plate and chill for 24 hours.

Unmould the cheesecake on to a plate and decorate with cherries and angelica.
Serves 6

OLD ENGLISH GOOSEBERRY CHEESECAKE

METRIC/IMPERIAL	AMERICAN
Base	*Base*
150 g/5 oz shortbread biscuits, crushed	1¼ cups crushed shortcake cookies
1 teaspoon ground mixed spice	1 teaspoon ground apple pie spice
65 g/2½ oz butter, melted	5 tablespoons butter, melted
Filling	*Filling*
750 g/1½ lb gooseberries	4 cups gooseberries
175 g/6 oz caster sugar	¾ cup sugar
5 teaspoons gelatine	5 teaspoons unflavored gelatin
2 tablespoons water	2 tablespoons water
350 g/12 oz cream cheese	1½ cups cream cheese
300 ml/½ pint double cream	1¼ cups heavy cream
¼ teaspoon arrowroot	¼ teaspoon arrowroot

Mix together the biscuit (cookie) crumbs, spice and butter and press over the bottom of a greased 20 cm/8 inch loose-bottomed cake tin (springform pan). Chill the base while preparing filling.

Place the gooseberries and sugar in a pan over a gentle heat and simmer to a pulp. Sieve to remove the pips.

Put the gelatine and water into a small heatproof bowl over a pan of hot water and stir until the gelatine has dissolved. Stir the gelatine into 450 ml/¾ pint of the gooseberry purée; leave to cool.

Beat the cream cheese until smooth and beat in the gooseberry mixture. Whip the cream and fold it in. Spoon the mixture into the prepared pan and chill until set.

Mix the arrowroot with the remaining gooseberry purée and boil until thickened. Cool, then spoon over the top of the cheesecake. Chill until set.
Serves 8

SUNSHINE YOGURT CHEESECAKE

METRIC/IMPERIAL	AMERICAN
200 g/7 oz coconut biscuits, crushed	1¾ cups crushed coconut cookies
75 g/3 oz butter, melted	6 tablespoons butter
225 g/8 oz curd cheese	1 cup curd cheese
150 ml/¼ pint plain yogurt	⅔ cup plain yogurt
4 tablespoons clear honey	4 tablespoons honey
2 oranges	2 oranges
15 g/½ oz gelatine	1 envelope unflavored gelatin

Mix together the biscuit (cookie) crumbs and butter and press over the bottom and up the sides of a greased 21.5 cm/8½ inch china flan dish. Chill the base while preparing filling.

Beat the cheese, yogurt and honey together until smooth. Grate the rind from both oranges and add to the cheese mixture. Squeeze the juice from one orange and place it in a saucepan with the gelatine. Dissolve over gentle heat, cool slightly and add to the cheese mixture. Pour into the prepared crumb case and chill until set. Remove the white pith from the remaining orange and cut out the segments. Arrange in a cartwheel pattern on top of the cheesecake.
Serves 8

Crunchy Rhubarb Cheesecake; Old English Gooseberry Cheesecake

CRUNCHY RHUBARB CHEESECAKE

METRIC/IMPERIAL	AMERICAN
Base	*Base*
50 g/2 oz margarine	¼ cup margarine
50 g/2 oz caster sugar	¼ cup sugar
1 tablespoon golden syrup	1 tablespoon light corn syrup
50 g/2 oz cornflakes, roughly crushed	2 cups cornflakes, roughly crushed
Filling	*Filling*
225 g/8 oz cream cheese	1 cup cream cheese
2 eggs, separated	2 eggs, separated
150 ml/¼ pint soured cream	⅔ cup sour cream
15 g/½ oz gelatine	1 envelope unflavored gelatin
1 × 539 g/1 lb 3 oz can rhubarb	1 can (1¼ lb) rhubarb
50 g/2 oz caster sugar	¼ cup sugar
Topping	*Topping*
2 teaspoons gelatine	2 teaspoons unflavored gelatin
few drops of red food colouring	few drops of red food coloring

Melt the margarine in a saucepan. Stir in the sugar and syrup. Remove pan and stir in the cornflakes. Press the mixture over the bottom of a greased 20 cm/8 inch loose-bottomed cake tin (springform pan). Chill the base while preparing filling.

Beat together the cream cheese, egg yolks and soured cream until smooth. Place the gelatine and 4 tablespoons syrup from the rhubarb into a small heatproof bowl over a pan of hot water and stir until the gelatine has dissolved. Stir gelatine into the cheese mixture. Stiffly whisk the egg whites and whisk in the sugar until stiff. Fold into the cheese mixture. Spoon into the prepared pan and chill until firm.

Drain the rhubarb. Dissolve the gelatine for the topping in the remaining rhubarb syrup over a low heat. Add a few drops of colouring and chill. Arrange the rhubarb on top of the cheesecake and, when the topping is on the point of setting, spoon it over the rhubarb. Chill for several hours, then remove the cheesecake from the pan to a plate for serving.
Serves 8 to 10

REDCURRANT CHEESE TART

METRIC/IMPERIAL	AMERICAN
1 × 25 cm/10 inch round sponge flan case	1 × 10 inch round sponge cake case
225 g/8 oz cream cheese	1 cup cream cheese
grated rind and juice of 1 lemon	grated rind and juice of 1 lemon
4 tablespoons single cream	4 tablespoons light cream
25 g/1 oz caster sugar	2 tablespoons sugar
450 g/1 lb redcurrants	4 cups red currants
225 g/8 oz redcurrant jelly	1 cup red currant jelly

Place the sponge case on a plate. Beat together the cream cheese, lemon rind, cream and sugar until smooth. Spread over the bottom of sponge case. Arrange the redcurrants on top.

Heat the redcurrant jelly and lemon juice together in a small pan until melted. Cool slightly then brush over the redcurrants. Serve chilled.
Serves 8 to 10

TANGY LIME CHEESECAKE

METRIC/IMPERIAL	AMERICAN
Base	*Base*
100 g/4 oz plain sweet biscuits, crushed	1 cup crushed plain sweet cookies
50 g/2 oz butter, melted	$\frac{1}{4}$ cup butter, melted
Filling	*Filling*
grated rind and juice of 2 limes	grated rind and juice of 2 limes
about 3 tablespoons lemon juice	about 3 tablespoons lemon juice
225 g/8 oz curd cheese	1 cup curd cheese
150 ml/$\frac{1}{4}$ pint sweetened condensed milk	$\frac{2}{3}$ cup sweetened condensed milk
To decorate	*For decoration*
fresh lime slices	fresh lime slices

Mix together the biscuit (cookie) crumbs and butter and press over the bottom of a greased 19 cm/7$\frac{1}{2}$ inch loose-bottomed fluted flan tin (pie pan). Chill the base while preparing filling.

Mix the lime juice with sufficient lemon juice to give 6 tablespoons in all. Place the juice, lime rind, curd cheese and condensed milk in a bowl and whisk together until smooth. Pour into the flan tin (pie pan) and chill for several hours until set. Remove from the pan and decorate with fresh lime slices. Serves 6

BLACKCURRANT TOPPED CHEESECAKE

METRIC/IMPERIAL	AMERICAN
Base	*Base*
200 g/7 oz digestive biscuits, crushed	1$\frac{3}{4}$ cups crushed graham crackers
90 g/3$\frac{1}{2}$ oz butter, melted	7 tablespoons butter, melted
Filling	*Filling*
1 × 350 g/12 oz can blackcurrants	1 × 12 oz can blackcurrants
15 g/$\frac{1}{2}$ oz gelatine	2 envelopes unflavored gelatin
juice of 1 small orange	juice of 1 small orange
175 g/6 oz cream cheese	$\frac{3}{4}$ cup cream cheese
2 eggs, separated	2 eggs, separated
50 g/2 oz caster sugar	$\frac{1}{4}$ cup sugar
200 ml/$\frac{1}{3}$ pint double cream, whipped	1 cup heavy cream
2 teaspoons arrowroot	2 teaspoons arrowroot

Mix together the biscuit (cracker) crumbs and butter and press over the bottom of a greased 18 cm/7 inch loose-bottomed cake tin (springform pan). Chill the base while preparing filling.

Drain the blackcurrants, reserving the syrup. Put the gelatine and orange juice into a small heatproof bowl over a pan of hot water and stir until the gelatine has dissolved.

Beat together the cream cheese, egg yolks and sugar. Stir in 4 tablespoons blackcurrant syrup and half the blackcurrants. Stir in the gelatine, then fold in the cream. Stiffly whisk the egg whites and fold into the mixture. Spoon the mixture into prepared pan and chill until set.

Stir the arrowroot with the remaining blackcurrant syrup in a small pan. Bring to the boil, stirring until thickened. Add the reserved blackcurrants and leave to cool. Spoon the topping over the cheesecake and chill until completely cold. Remove from the pan and serve.

Serves 8

QUICK 'N' EASY CHEESECAKE

METRIC/IMPERIAL	AMERICAN
450 g/1 lb cream cheese	2 cups cream cheese
50 g/2 oz caster sugar	$\frac{1}{4}$ cup sugar
300 ml/$\frac{1}{2}$ pint double cream	1$\frac{1}{4}$ cups heavy cream
1 × 298 g/10$\frac{1}{2}$ can mandarin orange segments in natural juice	1 × 11 oz can mandarin orange segments in natural juice
15 g/$\frac{1}{2}$ oz gelatine	1 envelope unflavored gelatin
100 g/4 oz digestive biscuits, crushed	1 cup crushed graham crackers
50 g/2 oz butter, melted	$\frac{1}{4}$ cup butter, melted
To decorate	*For decoration*
extra mandarin orange segments	extra mandarin orange segments

Beat together the cream cheese and sugar, then beat in the cream until smooth. Drain the mandarin oranges, reserving the juice. Put the gelatine and juice into a small heatproof bowl over a pan of hot water and stir until the gelatine has dissolved. Leave to cool slightly then stir into the cheese mixture with the mandarin oranges.

Pour the mixture into a greased and lined 20 cm/8 inch cake tin (baking pan) and chill until set. Mix the biscuit (cracker) crumbs with the butter and carefully press on top of the cheesecake. Chill for several hours.

Invert the cheesecake on to a serving plate and decorate with mandarin orange segments. Serves 8

BOOZY BANANA CHEESECAKE

METRIC/IMPERIAL	AMERICAN
75 g/3 oz gingernut biscuits, crushed	$\frac{3}{4}$ cup crushed gingersnap cookies
40 g/1$\frac{1}{2}$ oz butter, melted	3 tablespoons melted butter
40 g/1$\frac{1}{2}$ oz custard powder	6 tablespoons Bird's English dessert mix
75 g/3 oz caster sugar	6 tablespoons sugar
300 ml/$\frac{1}{2}$ pint milk	1$\frac{1}{4}$ cups milk
2 large ripe bananas	2 large ripe bananas
2 tablespoons dark rum	2 tablespoons dark rum
1 tablespoon lemon juice	1 tablespoon lemon juice
75 g/3 oz cream cheese	3 oz cream cheese
Topping	*Topping*
whipped cream	whipped cream
1 banana, sliced	1 banana, sliced
a little lemon juice	a little lemon juice

Mix together the biscuit (cookie) crumbs and butter and press over the bottom of a greased 19 cm/7$\frac{1}{2}$ inch loose-bottomed fluted flan tin (pie pan). Chill the base while preparing filling.

Mix together the custard powder (dessert mix) and 50 g/2 oz ($\frac{1}{4}$ cup) sugar. Make up the custard (dessert mix) in the usual way with the milk, stirring all the time as it becomes very thick. Mash the bananas with the remaining sugar, rum and lemon juice. Beat the bananas into the custard, then beat in the cream cheese until smooth. Spread on base and chill until set.

Remove the cheesecake from the tin and decorate with swirls of cream and banana slices, dipped in lemon juice. Serves 6

Boozy Banana Cheesecake; Tangy Lime Cheesecake

PEACH CHEESECAKE SANDWICH

METRIC/IMPERIAL	AMERICAN
1 × 142 g/5 oz packets peach table jelly	1 package peach-flavored gelatin
4 tablespoons water	4 tablespoons water
2 eggs, separated	2 eggs, separated
5 tablespoons milk	$\frac{2}{3}$ cup milk
grated rind and juice of $\frac{1}{2}$ lemon	grated rind and juice of $\frac{1}{2}$ lemon
15 g/$\frac{1}{2}$ oz caster sugar	1 tablespoon sugar
1 × 18 cm/7 inch round sponge cake (bought or homemade)	1 × 7 inch round sponge cake (bought or homemade)
225 g/8 oz cream cheese	1 cup cream cheese
150 ml/$\frac{1}{4}$ pint double cream	$\frac{2}{3}$ cup heavy cream
Topping	*Topping*
1 × 200 g/7oz can peach slices, drained	1 × 7 oz can peach slices, drained
icing sugar	confectioners' sugar

Cut the jelly (gelatin) into pieces and place in a saucepan with the water. Place over a gentle heat and stir until dissolved. Whisk the egg yolks with the milk, then add to the jelly (gelatin). Return the jelly (gelatin) mixture to the heat and stir for 2 minutes without boiling. Stir in the lemon rind, juice and sugar. Leave to cool until on the point of setting.

Split the sponge cake in half, and place one half in a greased 18 cm/7 inch loose-bottomed cake tin (springform pan). Whisk the cream cheese until smooth and whisk in the jelly (gelatin) mixture, a little at a time. Lightly whisk the cream and fold into the cheese mixture. Whisk the egg whites until stiff and fold into the mixture. Spoon into the prepared pan. Top with the remaining sponge cake half and chill for several hours.

Remove the cheesecake from the pan and decorate with the peach slices and icing (confectioners') sugar.
Serves 8

SWISS APPLE CHEESECAKE

METRIC/IMPERIAL	AMERICAN
1 tablespoon lemon juice	1 tablespoon lemon juice
250 ml/8 fl oz water	1 cup water
50 g/2 oz caster sugar	$\frac{1}{4}$ cup sugar
3 large dessert apples	3 large dessert apples
1 tablespoon gelatine	1 tablespoon unflavored gelatin
350 g/12 oz cottage cheese, sieved	1$\frac{1}{2}$ cups cottage cheese, sieved
$\frac{1}{2}$ teaspoon ground cinnamon	$\frac{1}{2}$ teaspoon ground cinnamon
25 g/1 oz raisins	$\frac{1}{4}$ cup raisins
120 ml/4 fl oz double cream	$\frac{1}{2}$ cup heavy cream
1 egg white	1 egg white
50 g/2 oz caster sugar	$\frac{1}{4}$ cup sugar
2 tablespoons apricot jam, sieved	2 tablespoons apricot jam, strained

Put the lemon juice, water and sugar into a large shallow pan and heat gently to dissolve the sugar. Core and cut each apple into 16 slices. Poach the apple slices in the syrup for 5 to 6 minutes until just tender. Drain the apples, reserving the syrup, and leave to cool. Put the gelatine and 120 ml/4 fl oz ($\frac{1}{2}$ cup) of the reserved syrup into a small heatproof bowl over a pan of hot water and stir until the gelatine has dissolved.

Arrange half the apple slices in a decorative pattern over the bottom of a buttered 20 cm/8 inch loose-bottomed cake tin (springform pan). Mix together the cottage cheese, cinnamon, gelatine and raisins and chill until almost setting. Whip the cream. Stiffly whisk the egg white and whisk in the sugar. Fold the cream, and then the egg white into the cheese mixture. Spoon into the cake pan and smooth the top. Top with the remaining apple slices and press down gently. Cover and chill until set.

Remove the cheesecake from the pan. Warm the apricot jam in a small pan and brush over the apple slices to glaze.
Serves 6

Peach Cheesecake Sandwich; Swiss Apple Cheesecake

LUSCIOUS PINEAPPLE CHEESECAKE

METRIC/IMPERIAL	AMERICAN
Filling	*Filling*
1 × 794 g/1 lb 12 oz can crushed pineapple	2 × 14 oz cans crushed pineapple
25 g/1 oz gelatine	1 oz unflavored gelatin
6 tablespoons water	6 tablespoons water
350 g/12 oz cream cheese	1½ cups cream cheese
50 g/2 oz caster sugar	¼ cup sugar
300 ml/½ pint double cream	1¼ cups heavy cream
Base	*Base*
100 g/4 oz digestive biscuits, crushed	1 cup crushed graham crackers
50 g/2 oz butter, melted	¼ cup butter, melted
Topping	*Topping*
1 × 225 g/8 oz can pineapple rings	1 × ½ lb can pineapple rings
2 teaspoons arrowroot	2 teaspoons arrowroot

Place the crushed pineapple in a bowl. Put the gelatine and water into a small heatproof bowl over a pan of hot water and stir until the gelatine has dissolved. Stir into the pineapple and leave until cool and just setting.

Beat the cream cheese and sugar until smooth. Stir in the pineapple. Whisk the cream until it just holds its shape. Fold into the pineapple mixture. Spoon into a greased 18 cm/7 inch loose-bottomed cake tin (springform pan). Mix the biscuit (cracker) crumbs with the butter and sprinkle over the cheesecake, pressing down gently with a palette knife. Cover and refrigerate until set.

Invert the cheesecake on to a serving plate and remove the pan. Drain the pineapple rings and reserve 150 ml/¼ pint (⅔ cup) of the syrup. Mix the arrowroot and reserved syrup together in a small pan and bring to the boil, stirring. Arrange the pineapple rings on top of the cheesecake and brush with the glaze.

Serves 8

RED PLUM CHEESECAKE

METRIC/IMPERIAL	AMERICAN
450 g/1 lb cottage cheese	2 cups cottage cheese
175 g/6 oz caster sugar	¾ cup sugar
1 × 450 g/15.9 oz carton plum yogurt	2 cups plum yogurt
2 tablespoons gelatine	2 tablespoons unflavored gelatin
4 tablespoons port wine	4 tablespoons port wine
1 Swiss roll	1 jelly roll
To decorate	*For decoration*
fresh red plums	fresh red plums

Sieve the cottage cheese. Mix the cottage cheese with the sugar and plum yogurt. Put the gelatine and port into a small heatproof bowl over a pan of hot water and stir until the gelatine has dissolved. Cool and stir into the cheese mixture. Pour the mixture into a greased 1.5 litre/2½ pint (1½ quart) ring mould and chill until just setting.

Cut the Swiss (jelly) roll into slices and press on top of the cheesecake. Chill again until set.

Invert the cheesecake on to a serving plate. Fill the centre with plum slices.

Serves 8

UNCOOKED SWEET CHEESECAKES

Flavourings for the delectable cheesecakes in this chapter include chocolate, coffee, liqueurs, nuts and honey.

BUTTERSCOTCH CHEESECAKE

METRIC/IMPERIAL

Base
40 g/1½ oz butter
40 g/1½ oz plain chocolate
1½ tablespoons golden syrup
175 g/6 oz rolled oats, toasted

Filling
25 g/1 oz butter
2 tablespoons golden syrup
4 tablespoons light soft brown sugar
150 ml/¼ pint boiling water
few drops of lemon juice
15 g/½ oz gelatine
225 g/8 oz full fat soft cheese
2 eggs, separated
25 g/1 oz caster sugar
1 × 170 g/6 oz can evaporated milk, chilled

To decorate
150 ml/¼ pint double or whipping cream

AMERICAN

Base
3 tablespoons butter
1½ squares (1 oz each) semi-sweet chocolate
1½ tablespoons light corn syrup
1¾ cups rolled oats, toasted

Filling
2 tablespoons butter
2 tablespoons corn syrup
¼ cup firmly packed light brown sugar
¾ cup boiling water
few drops of lemon juice
1 envelope unflavored gelatin
1 package (8 oz) cream cheese
2 eggs, separated
2 tablespoons sugar
1 × 6 oz can evaporated milk, chilled

For decoration
¾ cup whipping cream

First make the base: slowly melt the butter, chocolate and syrup in a pan and stir in the toasted rolled oats. Reserve 3 tablespoons of the oat mixture for decoration. Press the remaining oat mixture over the bottom of a greased 20 cm/8 inch loose-bottomed cake tin (springform pan). Chill the base while preparing filling.

Melt the butter, syrup and brown sugar in a pan. Boil until a rich caramel colour, remove from the heat and carefully stir in the water and lemon juice. Sprinkle over the gelatine and stir until dissolved. Leave to cool but not set.

Meanwhile soften the cheese in a large bowl and beat in the egg yolks and sugar. Whisk the evaporated milk until softly peaking and fold into the cheese mixture with the cool butterscotch sauce. Leave until the mixture starts to thicken. Whisk the egg whites until stiff and lightly fold into the butterscotch mixture. Pour into prepared tin and smooth the top. Leave in the refrigerator to set.

If necessary, run a knife around inside of tin, then remove cheesecake. Crumble reserved oat mixture and spoon a border around top of cheesecake. Whip the cream until softly peaking and swirl on top of the cheesecake.
Serves 6 to 8

TOASTED HAZELNUT CHEESECAKE

METRIC/IMPERIAL	AMERICAN
65 g/2½ oz butter	5 tablespoons butter
100 g/4 oz digestive biscuits, crushed	1 cup crushed graham crackers
75 g/3 oz toasted hazelnuts, chopped	¾ cup chopped toasted hazelnuts
225 g/8 oz full fat soft cheese	1 × ½ lb package cream cheese
2 eggs, separated	2 eggs, separated
100 g/4 oz caster sugar	½ cup sugar
150 ml/¼ pint double cream	¾ cup heavy cream
150 g/5 oz hazelnut yogurt	¾ cup hazelnut-flavored yogurt
15 g/½ oz gelatine	1 envelope unflavored gelatin
4 tablespoons water	¼ cup water
To decorate	*For decoration*
whipped cream	whipped cream
whole hazelnuts	whole hazelnuts

Melt the butter in a pan and stir in the biscuit (cracker) crumbs and 25 g/1 oz (¼ cup) of the chopped nuts. Press the crumb mixture over the bottom of a greased 20 cm/8 inch loose-bottomed cake tin (springform pan). Chill the base while preparing filling.

Soften the cheese in a large bowl and beat in the egg yolks, sugar, cream and yogurt.

Put the gelatine and water in a small heatproof bowl over a pan of hot water and stir until the gelatine has dissolved. Leave to cool slightly then stir the gelatine into the cheese mixture. Leave until the mixture starts to thicken. Whisk the egg whites until stiff and lightly fold into the cheese mixture with the remaining hazelnuts. Pour into prepared tin and smooth the top.

If necessary, run a knife around inside of tin, then remove cheesecake. Decorate with swirls of piped whipped cream and whole hazelnuts.
Serves 6 to 8

COFFEE CREAM CHEESECAKE

METRIC/IMPERIAL	AMERICAN
50 g/2 oz butter or margarine	¼ cup butter or margarine
1 tablespoon golden syrup	1 tablespoon light corn syrup
75 g/3 oz cornflakes, crushed	1½ cups crushed cornflakes
2 eggs, separated	2 eggs, separated
75 g/3 oz caster sugar	6 tablespoons sugar
2 tablespoons instant coffee powder	2 tablespoons instant coffee powder
150 ml/¼ pint milk	¾ cup milk
15 g/½ oz gelatine	1 envelope unflavored gelatin
4 tablespoons water	¼ cup water
225 g/8 oz cottage cheese, sieved	1 cup sieved cottage cheese
150 ml/¼ pint double or whipping cream	½ cup whipping cream
Topping	*Topping*
150 ml/¼ pint double or whipping cream	¾ cup whipping cream
1 tablespoon coffee liqueur (optional)	1 tablespoon coffee liqueur (optional)
few walnut halves	few walnut halves

Melt the butter or margarine and syrup in a pan and stir in the crushed cornflakes. Press the mixture over the bottom of a greased 20 cm/8 inch loose-bottomed cake tin (springform pan). Chill the base while preparing filling.

Whisk the egg yolks, sugar and coffee together. Gradually add the milk and pour into a pan. Heat gently, stirring continuously, until the mixture thickens slightly. Cover and leave to cool.

Put the gelatine and water into a small heatproof bowl over a pan of hot water and stir until the gelatine has dissolved. Leave until cool but not set. Stir into the coffee custard.

Soften the cottage cheese in a large bowl and beat in the cream and coffee custard. Leave until the mixture starts to thicken. Whisk the egg whites until stiff and lightly fold into cheese mixture. Pour into prepared tin and smooth the top. Leave in refrigerator to set.

If necessary, run a knife around inside of tin then remove cheesecake. Whip the cream and liqueur, if using, together until thick. Pipe a border around cheesecake and decorate with walnut halves.
Serves 6 to 8

Toasted Hazelnut Cheesecake; Coffee Cream Cheesecake

CHEESECAKE BRÛLÉE

METRIC/IMPERIAL	AMERICAN
1 sponge layer, 22 cm/8½ inches in diameter and 1 cm/½ inch thick	1 sponge cake layer, 8½ inches in diameter and ½ inch thick
225 g/8 oz cottage cheese, sieved	1 cup sieved cottage cheese
75 g/3 oz caster sugar	6 tablespoons sugar
3 eggs	3 eggs
15 g/½ oz gelatine	1 envelope unflavored gelatin
4 tablespoons water	¼ cup water
300 ml/½ pint double cream	1¼ cups heavy cream
1 teaspoon vanilla essence	1 teaspoon vanilla
40 g/1½ oz demerara sugar	¼ cup raw brown sugar
To decorate	*For decoration*
whipped cream	whipped cream

Press the sponge cake layer into the bottom of a greased 20 cm/8 inch loose-bottomed cake tin (springform pan).

Soften the cottage cheese in a large bowl, add the white sugar and beat well. Add the eggs one at a time, beating well after each addition.

Put the gelatine and water into a small heatproof bowl over a pan of hot water and stir until the gelatine has dissolved. Leave until cool but not set.

Stir the gelatine into the cheese mixture. Leave until mixture starts to thicken. Whip the cream and vanilla together until softly peaking and fold into the cheese mixture. Pour over the sponge base and smooth the top. Leave in refrigerator to set and become very cold.

Sprinkle surface evenly with brown sugar and place under a preheated very hot grill (broiler) for a minute or two until the sugar melts and browns to form a caramel glaze (the cheesecake mixture may melt slightly but this will set again on chilling). Leave to cool then chill for 2 hours or overnight.

If necessary, run a knife around inside of tin then remove cheesecake. Decorate with a border of piped whipped cream.
Serves 6 to 8

MARSHMALLOW CHEESECAKE RING

METRIC/IMPERIAL	AMERICAN
175 g/6 oz marshmallows	24 large marshmallows
2 tablespoons milk	2 tablespoons milk
100 g/4 oz soft dark brown sugar	⅔ cup dark brown sugar
100 g/4 oz full fat soft cheese	1 × ¼ lb package cream cheese
100 g/4 oz cottage cheese, sieved	½ cup sieved cottage cheese
2 eggs, separated	2 eggs, separated
½ teaspoon vanilla essence	½ teaspoon vanilla
1 × 150 g/5 oz carton natural yogurt	¾ cup plain yogurt
15 g/½ oz gelatine	1 envelope unflavored gelatin
5 tablespoons water	5 tablespoons water
40 g/1½ oz butter	3 tablespoons butter
75 g/3 oz Nice biscuits, crushed	¾ cup crushed plain sweet cookies
To decorate	*For decoration*
50 g/2 oz blanched almonds, toasted	½ cup blanched almonds, toasted
150 ml/¼ pint whipped cream	¾ cup whipped cream

Place the marshmallows, milk and sugar in a pan and stir over a gentle heat until the marshmallows have melted and the sugar has dissolved. Remove from the heat and beat until smooth.

Soften the cheeses in a large bowl and beat in the egg yolks, melted marshmallow mixture, vanilla and yogurt.

Put the gelatine and water into a small heatproof bowl over a pan of hot water and stir until the gelatine has dissolved. Leave until cool but not set.

Stir the gelatine into the cheese mixture. Leave until the mixture starts to thicken. Whisk the egg whites until stiff and fold into the cheese mixture. Spoon into a well greased 20 cm/8 inch ring mould. Leave in the refrigerator to set.

Melt the butter in a pan and stir in the biscuit (cookie) crumbs. Sprinkle evenly over the almost set cheesecake mixture and press lightly with the back of a metal spoon. Leave in the refrigerator until completely set.

Just before serving, ease the cheesecake away from the sides of the mould and invert the set cheesecake on to a serving plate. Decorate with cream and nuts.
Serves 6 to 8

SUGAR AND SPICE CHEESECAKE

METRIC/IMPERIAL	AMERICAN
90 g/3½ oz butter or margarine	7 tablespoons butter or margarine
1 × 200 g/7.05 oz packet spicy fruit biscuits, crushed	2 cups crushed spicy dried fruit cookies
good pinch of ground mixed spice	⅛ teaspoon apple pie spice
Filling	*Filling*
225 g/8 oz cottage cheese, sieved	1 cup sieved cottage cheese
1 × 397 g/14 oz can sweetened condensed milk	1 × 1 lb can sweetened condensed milk
finely grated rind of 1 large lemon	finely grated rind of 1 large lemon
juice of 2 large lemons	juice of 2 large lemons
good pinch of ground ginger	⅛ teaspoon ground ginger
½ teaspoon ground cinnamon	½ teaspoon ground cinnamon
½ teaspoon ground mixed spice	½ teaspoon apple pie spice
To decorate	*For decoration*
1 tablespoon icing sugar	1 tablespoon confectioners' sugar
1 teaspoon ground cinnamon	1 teaspoon ground cinnamon

Melt the butter or margarine in a pan and stir in the biscuit (cookie) crumbs and spice. Press the crumb mixture over the bottom and 3.5 cm/1½ inches up the sides of a greased 20 cm/8 inch loose-bottomed cake tin (springform pan). Chill the base while preparing filling.

Soften the cheese in a large bowl. Beat in the condensed milk, lemon rind and juice and spices until the mixture thickens. Pour into the prepared tin and smooth the top. Leave in the refrigerator to set.

Run a knife around inside of tin then remove cheesecake. Neaten the top edges of crumb case. Sprinkle with a mixture of icing (confectioners') sugar and cinnamon which will dissolve to give a spicy brown top to the cheesecake.
Serves 6 to 8

SOUR CREAM AND HONEY CHEESECAKE

METRIC/IMPERIAL	AMERICAN
50 g/2 oz butter	$\frac{1}{4}$ cup butter
4 tablespoons clear honey	$\frac{1}{4}$ cup honey
150 g/5 oz oatcake biscuits, crushed	$1\frac{1}{4}$ cups crushed oaty cookies
225 g/8 oz full fat soft cheese	$1 \times \frac{1}{2}$ lb package cream cheese
2 eggs, separated	2 eggs, separated
50 g/2 oz caster sugar	$\frac{1}{4}$ cup sugar
1 × 142 ml/5 fl oz carton soured cream	$\frac{3}{4}$ cup sour cream
15 g/$\frac{1}{2}$ oz gelatine	1 envelope unflavored gelatin
4 tablespoons water	$\frac{1}{4}$ cup water
Topping	*Topping*
$1\frac{1}{2}$ tablespoons clear honey	$1\frac{1}{2}$ tablespoons honey
40 g/$1\frac{1}{2}$ oz walnuts, roughly chopped	$\frac{1}{3}$ cup roughly chopped walnuts

Melt the butter and 1 tablespoon of the honey in a pan and stir in the oatcake (cookie) crumbs. Press the crumb mixture over the bottom of a greased 20 cm/8 inch loose-bottomed cake tin (springform pan). Chill the base while preparing filling.

Soften the cheese in a large bowl, beat in the egg yolks, sugar, soured cream and remaining honey.

Put the gelatine and water into a small heatproof bowl over a pan of hot water and stir until the gelatine has dissolved. Leave until cool but not set.

Stir the gelatine into the cheese mixture and leave until the mixture starts to thicken. Whisk the egg whites until stiff and fold lightly into the cheese mixture. Pour into the prepared tin and smooth the top. Leave in the refrigerator to set.

If necessary, run a knife around inside of tin then remove cheesecake. Mix the honey and nuts together and spoon a border around top of cheesecake.
Serves 6 to 8

Cheesecake Brûlée; Marshmallow Cheesecake Ring

PINA COLADA CHEESECAKE

METRIC/IMPERIAL	AMERICAN
75 g/3 oz butter	6 tablespoons butter
150 g/5 oz Nice biscuits, crushed	1¼ cups crushed plain sweet cookies
50 g/2 oz desiccated coconut, toasted	⅔ cup shredded coconut, toasted
225 g/8 oz full fat soft cheese	1 × ½ lb package cream cheese
2 eggs, separated	2 eggs, separated
75 g/3 oz caster sugar	6 tablespoons sugar
15 g/½ oz gelatine	1 envelope unflavored gelatin
5 tablespoons unsweetened pineapple juice	5 tablespoons unsweetened pineapple juice
3–4 tablespoons Malibu	3–4 tablespoons Malibu
150 ml/¼ pint double or whipping cream	¾ cup whipping cream
Topping	*Topping*
whipped cream	whipped cream
few cocktail cherries	maraschino cherries
toasted desiccated coconut	toasted shredded coconut

Melt the butter in a pan and stir in the biscuit (cookie) crumbs and coconut. Press the crumb mixture over the bottom of a greased 20 cm/8 inch loose-bottomed cake tin and chill.

Soften the cheese in a large bowl and beat in the egg yolks and sugar. Put the gelatine, pineapple juice and Malibu into a small heatproof bowl over a pan of hot water and stir until the gelatine has dissolved. Leave until cool but not set.

Stir the gelatine into the cheese mixture and leave until the mixture starts to thicken. Whisk the cream and egg whites until stiff and lightly fold alternately into the cheese mixture. Pour into the prepared tin and smooth the top. Leave in the refrigerator to set.

Run a knife around inside of tin then remove cheesecake. Decorate with swirls of cream, cherries and coconut.
Serves 6 to 8

CHOCOLATE RIPPLE CHEESECAKE

METRIC/IMPERIAL	AMERICAN
Base	*Base*
100 g/4 oz butter	½ cup butter
50 g/2 oz caster sugar	¼ cup sugar
225 g/8 oz digestive biscuits, crushed	2 cups crushed graham crackers
Filling	*Filling*
50 g/2 oz plain chocolate	2 squares (1 oz each) semisweet chocolate
knob of butter	pat of butter
120 ml/4 fl oz water	½ cup water
1 tablespoon golden syrup	1 tablespoon light corn syrup
few drops of vanilla essence	few drops of vanilla
450 g/1 lb full fat soft cheese	2 × 8 oz packages cream cheese
4 eggs, separated	4 eggs, separated
225 g/8 oz caster sugar	1 cup sugar
25 g/1 oz gelatine	2 envelopes unflavored gelatin
2 tablespoons sherry	2 tablespoons sherry
300 ml/½ pint double or whipping cream	1¼ cups whipping cream
Topping	*Topping*
whipped cream	whipped cream

Chocolate Ripple Cheesecake; Pina Colada Cheesecake

Melt the butter in a pan and stir in the sugar and biscuit (cracker) crumbs. Press the crumb mixture over the bottom of a greased 28 cm/11 inch loose-bottomed cake tin (springform pan). Chill the base while preparing filling.

Melt the chocolate and butter in a small heatproof bowl over a pan of hot water. Stir in 1 tablespoon of the water, the syrup and vanilla. Remove from the heat.

Soften the cheese in a large bowl and beat in the egg yolks and sugar. Put the gelatine, sherry and remaining water into a small heatproof bowl over a pan of hot water and stir until the gelatine has dissolved. Leave until cool but not set. Stir the gelatine into the cheese mixture. Leave until the mixture starts to thicken. Whisk the cream and egg whites until stiff and fold lightly but thoroughly into the cheese mixture. Pour into the prepared tin. Quickly drizzle the chocolate sauce over the cheesecake and swirl with a skewer to give a rippled effect. Tap the tin gently to level the surface. Leave in the refrigerator to set.

If necessary, run a knife around inside the tin then remove cheesecake. Decorate with a border of piped whipped cream.
Serves 10 to 12

JAMAICAN RUM CHEESECAKE

METRIC/IMPERIAL	AMERICAN
4–5 tablespoons dark rum	4–5 tablespoons dark rum
100 g/4 oz seedless raisins	$\frac{2}{3}$ cup raisins
50 g/2 oz butter or margarine	$\frac{1}{4}$ cup butter or margarine
150 g/5 oz dark brown sugar	1 cup dark brown sugar
150 g/5 oz gingernut biscuits, crushed	$1\frac{1}{4}$ cups crushed gingersnap cookies
100 g/4 oz cottage cheese	$\frac{1}{2}$ cup cottage cheese
100 g/4 oz full fat soft cheese	$1 \times \frac{1}{4}$ lb package cream cheese
2 eggs, separated	2 eggs, separated
1 × 150 g/5 oz carton natural yogurt	$\frac{3}{4}$ cup plain yogurt
15 g/$\frac{1}{2}$ oz gelatine	1 envelope unflavored gelatin
4 tablespoons water	$\frac{1}{4}$ cup water
Topping	*Topping*
15 g/$\frac{1}{2}$ oz plain cooking chocolate	$\frac{1}{2}$ 1-oz square semisweet chocolate
25 g/1 oz seedless raisins	3 tablespoons seedless raisins
whipped cream	whipped cream

Pour the rum over the raisins and leave to soak for at least 30 minutes, stirring occasionally.

Melt the butter or margarine in a pan and stir in 25 g/1 oz (3 tablespoons) of the sugar and the biscuit (cookie) crumbs. Press the crumb mixture over the bottom of a greased 20 cm/8 inch loose-bottomed cake tin (springform pan). Chill the base while preparing filling.

Soften the cheeses in a large bowl and beat in the egg yolks, remaining sugar and yogurt. Strain the raisins, reserving the rum. Stir the rum into the cheese mixture.

Put the gelatine and water into a small heatproof bowl over a pan of hot water and stir until the gelatine has dissolved. Leave until cool but not set. Stir the gelatine into the cheese mixture. Leave until the mixture starts to thicken. Whisk the egg whites until stiff and lightly but thoroughly fold into the cheese mixture with the reserved raisins. Pour into the prepared tin and smooth over the top. Leave in the refrigerator to set.

Meanwhile melt the chocolate in a heatproof bowl over hot water, add the raisins and mix well together. Drop small teaspoonfuls of chocolate raisin clusters on to greaseproof (parchment) paper and leave to set.

If necessary, run a knife around inside of tin then remove the cheesecake. Decorate with piped whipped cream and the chocolate raisin clusters.

Serves 6 to 8

CHESTNUT CHEESECAKE

METRIC/IMPERIAL
75 g/3 oz butter
25 g/1 oz caster sugar
175 g/6 oz digestive biscuits,
    crushed
1 × 425 g/15 oz can
    unsweetened chestnut
    purée
300 ml/½ pint double cream
225 g/8 oz full fat soft cheese
100 g/4 oz icing sugar,
    sieved
2 eggs
15 g/½ oz gelatine
juice of 1 lemon
Topping
1 × 142 ml/5 fl oz carton
    soured cream
chocolate curls

AMERICAN
6 tablespoons butter
2 tablespoons sugar
1½ cups crushed graham
    crackers
1 × 1 lb can unsweetened
    chestnut purée
1¼ cups heavy cream
1 × ½ lb package cream
    cheese
1 cup confectioners' sugar,
    sifted
2 eggs
1 envelope unflavored
    gelatin
juice of 1 lemon
Topping
¾ cup sour cream
chocolate curls

Melt the butter in a pan and stir in the sugar and biscuit (cracker) crumbs. Press the mixture over the bottom of a greased 20 cm/8 inch loose-bottomed cake tin and chill.

Mash the chestnut purée in a bowl and gradually beat in the cream. Soften the cheese in a large bowl and beat in the icing (confectioners') sugar. Add the eggs, one at a time, whisking well after each addition. Fold in the chestnut mixture.

Put the gelatine and lemon juice in a small heatproof bowl over a pan of hot water and stir until the gelatine has dissolved. Leave until cool but not set. Stir the gelatine into the cheese mixture and leave until it starts to thicken. Pour into prepared tin and smooth over top. Chill until set.

If necessary, run a knife around inside of tin then remove the cheesecake. Spread the sour cream over the cheesecake and decorate with chocolate curls.
Serves 6 to 8

Mocha and Vanilla Cheesecake; Crème de Menthe Cheesecake

SWEET SHERRY CHEESECAKE

METRIC/IMPERIAL	AMERICAN
50 g/2 oz butter	$\frac{1}{4}$ cup butter
150 g/5 oz caster sugar	$\frac{1}{2}$ cup plus 2 tablespoons sugar
150 g/5 oz milk chocolate wheatmeal biscuits, crushed	$1\frac{1}{4}$ cups crushed chocolate-coated graham crackers
225 g/8 oz full fat soft cheese	$1 \times \frac{1}{2}$ lb package cream cheese
2 eggs, separated	2 eggs, separated
150 ml/$\frac{1}{4}$ pint double or whipping cream	$\frac{3}{4}$ cup whipping cream
15 g/$\frac{1}{2}$ oz gelatine	1 envelope unflavored gelatin
juice of 1 medium lemon	juice of 1 medium-size lemon
4–5 tablespoons sweet sherry	4–5 tablespoons sweet sherry
Topping	*Topping*
whipped cream	whipped cream
few ratafias	few ratafias

Melt the butter in a pan and stir in 25 g/1 oz (2 tablespoons) of the sugar and the biscuit (cracker) crumbs. Press the crumb mixture over the bottom of a greased 20 cm/8 inch loose-bottomed cake tin (springform pan). Chill the base while preparing filling.

Soften the cheese in a large bowl and beat in the egg yolks, remaining sugar and cream. Put the gelatine and lemon juice into a small heatproof bowl over a pan of hot water and stir until the gelatine has dissolved. Stir in the sweet sherry and leave until cool but not set. Stir the gelatine into the cheese mixture and leave until the mixture starts to thicken. Whisk the egg whites until stiff and lightly fold into the cheese mixture. Pour into the prepared tin and smooth over the top. Leave in the refrigerator to set.

If necessary, run a knife around inside of tin then remove cheesecake. Decorate with piped whipped cream and ratafias.

Serves 6 to 8

CRÈME DE MENTHE CHEESECAKE

METRIC/IMPERIAL	AMERICAN
Base	*Base*
100 g/4 oz butter	$\frac{1}{2}$ cup butter
250 g/9 oz plain chocolate wheatmeal biscuits, crushed	$2\frac{1}{4}$ cups crushed chocolate-covered graham crackers
Filling	*Filling*
225 g/8 oz full fat soft cheese	$1 \times \frac{1}{2}$ lb package cream cheese
2 eggs, separated	2 eggs, separated
100 g/4 oz icing sugar, sieved	1 cup convectioners' sugar, sifted
150 ml/$\frac{1}{4}$ pint double or whipping cream	$\frac{3}{4}$ cup whipping cream
15 g/$\frac{1}{2}$ oz gelatine	1 envelope unflavored gelatin
2 tablespoons water	2 tablespoons water
3 tablespoons crème de menthe	3 tablespoons crème de menthe
few drops green food colouring	few drops green food coloring
Topping	*Topping*
whipped cream	whipped cream
few wafer thin chocolate mints	few wafer thin chocolate mints

Melt the butter in a pan and stir in the biscuit (cracker) crumbs. Press the crumb mixture evenly over the bottom and up the sides of a greased 20 cm/8 inch loose-bottomed cake tin (springform pan). Chill the base while preparing the filling.

Soften the cheese in a large bowl and beat in the egg yolks, icing (confectioners') sugar and cream. Put the gelatine, water and crème de menthe in a small heatproof bowl over a pan of hot water and stir until the gelatine has dissolved. Leave until cool but not set. Stir the gelatine into the cheese mixture. Mix in a few drops of green food colouring and leave until the mixture starts to thicken.

Whisk the egg whites until stiff and lightly but thoroughly fold into the cheese mixture, adding more food colouring if liked. Pour into prepared tin and chill until set.

Run a knife around inside of tin then remove the cheesecake. Decorate the top edge with piped whipped cream and halved wafer thin chocolate mints.

Serves 6 to 8

MOCHA AND VANILLA CHEESECAKE

METRIC/IMPERIAL	AMERICAN
50 g/2 oz butter	$\frac{1}{4}$ cup butter
100 g/4 oz shortcake biscuits, crushed	1 cup crushed shortbread cookies
225 g/8 oz full fat soft cheese	$1 \times \frac{1}{2}$ lb package cream cheese
2 eggs, separated	2 eggs, separated
100 g/4 oz caster sugar	$\frac{1}{2}$ cup sugar
150 ml/$\frac{1}{4}$ pint double or whipping cream	$\frac{3}{4}$ cup whipping cream
15 g/$\frac{1}{2}$ oz gelatine	1 envelope unflavored gelatin
4 tablespoons water	$\frac{1}{4}$ cup water
50 g/2 oz plain chocolate	2 squares (1 oz each) semisweet chocolate
2 tablespoons coffee essence	2 tablespoons coffee flavoring
$\frac{1}{2}$ teaspoon vanilla essence	$\frac{1}{2}$ teaspoon vanilla
Topping	*Topping*
whipped cream	whipped cream
coffee-flavoured chocolate beans	coffee-flavored chocolate beans

Melt the butter in a pan and stir in the biscuit (cookie) crumbs. Press the crumb mixture over the bottom of a greased 20 cm/8 inch loose-bottomed cake tin (springform pan). Chill the base while preparing filling.

Soften the cheese in a large bowl and beat in the egg yolks, sugar and cream. Put the gelatine and water in a small heatproof bowl over a pan of hot water and stir until the gelatine has dissolved. Leave until cool but not set.

Melt the chocolate in a small heatproof bowl over hot water and stir in the coffee essence (flavoring). Stir the gelatine into the cheese mixture. Divide the mixture in half and place in separate bowls. Add vanilla to one portion and the chocolate mixture to the other. Leave until both mixtures start to thicken.

Whisk the egg whites until stiff and lightly fold half the egg white into the vanilla mixture and pour into the prepared tin. Shake the tin gently to level the surface. Fold remaining egg white into mocha mixture and carefully spoon over vanilla layer. Smooth over surface with the back of a spoon. Leave in the refrigerator to set.

If necessary, run a knife around inside of tin then remove the cheesecake. Decorate with piped whipped cream and chocolate beans.

Serves 6 to 8

SWEET FLANS

An array of pastry tarts and sponge flans
with fillings that include fruit and custard
and classic treacle tart and Bakewell tart
recipes.

FRESH FRUIT FLAKY FLAN (PIE)

METRIC/IMPERIAL	AMERICAN
Flan case	*Pie shell*
225 g/8 oz plain flour	2 cups all-purpose flour
½ teaspoon salt	½ teaspoon salt
75 g/3 oz butter	6 tablespoons butter
75 g/3 oz lard	6 tablespoons shortening
about 7 tablespoons cold water, mixed with 1 tablespoon lemon juice	about 7 tablespoons cold water, mixed with 1 tablespoon lemon juice
beaten egg to glaze	beaten egg to glaze
Filling	*Filling*
3 peaches, skinned and sliced	3 peaches, skinned and sliced
2 bananas, peeled and sliced	2 bananas, peeled and sliced
100–175 g/4–6 oz black grapes, halved and seeded	about 1 cup halved and pitted purple grapes
4 tablespoons apricot jam	4 tablespoons apricot jam
1 tablespoon water	1 tablespoon water

Sift the flour and salt in a bowl. Blend the fats together into a
round and divide into four. Rub one quarter of the fat into the
flour with the fingertips until the mixture resembles fine
breadcrumbs. Add sufficient water and lemon juice to bind to
a soft dough. Knead lightly, cover and allow to rest in a cool
place for 20 minutes.

Roll out the dough to an oblong, about 5 mm/¼ inch thick,
three times as long as it is wide. With a knife, dot small knobs
of a second quarter of the fat over the top two-thirds of the
dough, leaving a 1 cm/½ inch border. Bring the bottom third of
the dough up and the top third down to cover the centre third.
Press the edges firmly with a rolling pin to seal. Allow the
dough to rest, uncovered, for a short while. Half turn the
dough, so that the fold is on the right. Repeat the rolling,
adding the fat and folding twice more. Cover and allow the
dough to rest in a cool place for at least 30 minutes before
using.

Roll out the dough to a rectangle 25 × 15 cm/10 × 6 inches.
Cut a 2.5 cm/1 inch strip off each side of rectangle. Place the
rectangle on a baking sheet and prick with a fork. Brush the
edges with beaten egg. Place the pastry strips on the edges of
the rectangle and press to seal. Leave to rest in a cool place
for 15 minutes. Mark a diamond pattern on the pastry border
with a knife and brush with egg. Cook in a preheated hot oven
(220°C/425°F, Gas Mark 7) for 15 to 20 minutes. Leave to cool
on a wire tray.

Arrange a line of peach slices down the centre of the flan
case (pie shell) with a line of banana slices and grape halves,
down either side. Heat the apricot jam with the water in a pan.
Bring to the boil and sieve. Brush over the fruit to glaze while
still warm. Serve with cream if liked.

Serves 6 to 8

GRAPEFRUIT MERINGUE FLAN (PIE)

METRIC/IMPERIAL	AMERICAN
Flan case	*Pie shell*
175 g/6 oz plain flour	1½ cups all-purpose flour
pinch of salt	pinch of salt
75 g/3 oz butter or block margarine and lard	6 tablespoons butter or margarine and shortening
2 tablespoons water	2 tablespoons water
Filling	*Filling*
grated rind and juice of 1 large grapefruit	grated rind and juice of 1 large grapefruit
2 tablespoons cornflour	2 tablespoons cornstarch
2 egg yolks, beaten	2 egg yolks, beaten
caster sugar to taste	sugar to taste
Meringue	*Meringue*
2 egg whites	2 egg whites
50 g/2 oz caster sugar	¼ cup sugar
halved glacé cherries to decorate	halved glacé cherries to decorate

Sift the flour and salt into a bowl. Rub (cut) in the fat until the mixture resembles fine breadcrumbs. Sprinkle over about 2 tablespoons water and stir together with a knife. Knead lightly into a smooth dough. Roll out the dough on a lightly floured surface and line an 18–20 cm/7–8 inch flan tin (pie pan). Line with greaseproof (parchment) paper and dried beans and 'bake blind' in a preheated moderately hot oven (200°C/400°F, Gas Mark 6) for 15 to 20 minutes.

Make the grapefruit juice up to 250 ml/8 fl oz (1 cup) with water. Place a little of the juice in a pan and blend in the cornflour (cornstarch). Add the remaining juice and the grapefruit rind and cook the sauce, stirring, for 2 minutes. Remove from the heat and beat in the egg yolks and sugar to taste. Pour the cooled filling into the cooled flan case (pie shell).

Whisk the egg whites until stiff, then gradually fold in the sugar. Spoon or pipe the meringue over the grapefruit filling. Decorate with the cherries.

Place in a moderately hot oven (200°C/400°F, Gas Mark 6) for about 10 minutes until the meringue is lightly browned.
Serves 4 to 6

Fresh Fruit Flaky Flan (Pie); French Apple Flan (Pie)

FRENCH APPLE FLAN (PIE)

METRIC/IMPERIAL	AMERICAN
Flan case	*Pie shell*
225 g/8 oz plain flour	2 cups all-purpose flour
pinch of salt	pinch of salt
100 g/4 oz caster sugar	½ cup sugar
100 g/4 oz butter	½ cup butter
3–4 egg yolks	3–4 egg yolks
Filling	*Filling*
1 kg/2 lb cooking apples, peeled, cored and chopped	2 lb tart apples, peeled, cored and chopped
about 100 g/4 oz sugar or to taste	about ½ cup sugar or to taste
25 g/1 oz butter	2 tablespoons butter
4 dessert apples, peeled, cored and quartered	4 eating apples, peeled, cored and quartered
1 tablespoon lemon juice	1 tablespoon lemon juice
3 tablespoons apricot jam, warmed and sieved	3 tablespoons apricot jam, warmed and sieved

Place the flour and salt on a working surface. Make a well in the centre and add the sugar, butter and egg yolks. Blend the ingredients together with the fingertips, gradually working in the flour. Add a little water, if necessary, to bind to a smooth dough. Allow to rest in a cool place for at least 30 minutes.

Roll out the dough on a lightly floured surface and line a 25 cm/10 inch flan tin (pie pan). Line with greaseproof (parchment) paper and dried beans and 'bake blind' in a preheated moderately hot oven (200°C/400°F, Gas Mark 6) for 10 minutes.

Place the chopped apples in a pan and cook, with a little water to prevent burning, until soft. Stir in the sugar to taste and butter and mix to make a purée. Slice the dessert (eating) apple quarters very thinly into half moon shapes. Toss the slices in the lemon juice and a little sugar.

Spread the apple purée in the pastry case (pie shell) and arrange the apple slices in overlapping circles on top.

Cook in a moderately hot oven (200°C/400°F, Gas Mark 6) for 30 to 40 minutes until the edges of the apple slices start to brown. Allow the flan to cool, then brush the surface with the warmed apricot jam.
Serves 8

MINCEMEAT AND APPLE FLAN (PIE)

METRIC/IMPERIAL	AMERICAN
Flan case	*Pie shell*
175 g/6 oz plain flour	1½ cups all-purpose flour
pinch of salt	pinch of salt
75 g/3 oz butter or block margarine and lard	6 tablespoons butter or margarine and shortening
1 tablespoon caster sugar	1 tablespoon sugar
2 tablespoons milk	2 tablespoons milk
Filling	*Filling*
1 large cooking apple, peeled and grated	1 large tart apple, peeled and grated
3 tablespoons caster sugar	3 tablespoons sugar
juice of ½ lemon	juice of ½ lemon
6–8 tablespoons mincemeat	6–8 tablespoons mincemeat
2 dessert apples, peeled, cored and quartered	2 eating apples, peeled, cored and quartered

Sift the flour and salt into a bowl. Rub (cut) in the fat until the mixture resembles fine breadcrumbs. Stir in the sugar. Sprinkle over the milk and stir together with a knife. Knead lightly to make a smooth dough.

Roll out the dough and line a 20 cm/8 inch fluted flan tin (pie pan). Spoon the grated apple into the base and sprinkle with half of the sugar and lemon juice. Liberally spread over the mincemeat to evenly cover the apple. Slice the quartered apples very thinly into half moon shapes. Toss the slices in the remaining sugar and lemon juice. Arrange the slices, overlapping, over the mincemeat in one circle around the edge. Cook in a preheated moderately hot oven (190°C/375°F, Gas Mark 5) for 35 to 40 minutes. Serve hot or cold.
Serves 4 to 6

Strawberry Sponge Flan (Pie); Hazelnut Tart

CHERRY AND ALMOND FLAN (PIE)

METRIC/IMPERIAL	AMERICAN
Flan case	*Pie shell*
175 g/6 oz plain flour	1½ cups all-purpose flour
pinch of salt	pinch of salt
75 g/3 oz butter	6 tablespoons butter
25 g/1 oz caster sugar	2 tablespoons sugar
1 egg yolk	1 egg yolk
Filling	*Filling*
450 g/1 lb fresh red cherries, stoned	1 lb fresh red cherries, pitted
65 g/2½ oz caster sugar	5 tablespoons sugar
50 g/2 oz butter	¼ cup butter
1 egg, beaten	1 egg, beaten
few drops of almond essence	few drops of almond extract
50 g/2 oz ground almonds	½ cup ground almonds
25 g/1 oz flaked almonds	2 tablespoons slivered almonds
To decorate	
fresh cherries	*For decoration*
	fresh cherries

Sift the flour and salt into a bowl. Rub (cut) in the butter until the mixture resembles fine breadcrumbs. Stir in the sugar. Add the egg yolk and stir together with a knife, adding a little water if necessary. Knead lightly to make a smooth dough. Leave to rest in a cool place for 30 minutes before using.

Roll out the dough and line a 20 cm/8 inch flan tin (pie pan). Line with greaseproof (parchment) paper and dried beans and 'bake blind' in a preheated moderately hot oven (200°C/400°F, Gas Mark 6) for 10 minutes.

Place the cherries in the flan case (pie shell) and sprinkle with 15 g/½ oz (1 tablespoon) of the sugar. Cream the butter and remaining sugar together until light and fluffy. Beat in the egg and almond essence (extract). Fold in the ground almonds. Spread this mixture evenly over the cherries. Sprinkle the flaked (slivered) almonds on top. Cook in a moderate oven (180°C/350°F, Gas Mark 4) for 35 minutes until golden. Serve hot or cold, decorated with fresh cherries.
Serves 4 to 6

STRAWBERRY SPONGE FLAN (PIE)

METRIC/IMPERIAL	AMERICAN
Sponge flan case	*Sponge cake case*
3 eggs	3 eggs
75 g/3 oz caster sugar	6 tablespoons sugar
75 g/3 oz plain flour	¾ cup all-purpose flour
½ teaspoon baking powder	½ teaspoon baking powder
Filling	*Filling*
about 450 g/1 lb strawberries, hulled	1 lb strawberries, hulled
4 tablespoons redcurrant jelly	4 tablespoons red currant jelly
1 tablespoon lemon juice	1 tablespoon lemon juice
2 tablespoons water	2 tablespoons water
To decorate	*For decoration*
whipped cream	whipped cream

Place the eggs and sugar in a large heatproof bowl over a pan of hot water. Whisk until the mixture is thick and light. Remove the bowl from the heat and whisk for 4 minutes to cool the mixture. Sift the flour and baking powder on to the whisked mixture and fold in using a metal spoon. Spoon the mixture into a lightly oiled and floured 20 cm/8 inch sponge flan tin. Cook in a preheated moderate oven (180°C/350°F, Gas Mark 4) for about 30 minutes. Cool on a wire tray.

Either halve or leave the strawberries whole. Arrange attractively, cut sides down, in the sponge cake case. Put the redcurrant jelly, lemon juice and water in a small pan and stir until the jelly has dissolved. Bring to the boil and boil until the glaze hangs from the spoon for a few seconds before dropping. Spoon the glaze over the fruit. Before serving, pipe rosettes of cream around the edge of the flan.
Serves 4 to 6

HAZELNUT TART

METRIC/IMPERIAL	AMERICAN
Flan case	*Pie shell*
175 g/6 oz plain flour	1½ cups all-purpose flour
pinch of salt	pinch of salt
75 g/3 oz butter	6 tablespoons butter
25 g/1 oz caster sugar	2 tablespoons sugar
1 egg yolk	1 egg yolk
Filling	*Filling*
3 tablespoons raspberry jam	3 tablespoons raspberry jam
100 g/4 oz butter	½ cup butter
100 g/4 oz caster sugar	½ cup sugar
½ teaspoon vanilla essence	½ teaspoon vanilla
2 eggs, beaten	2 eggs, beaten
100 g/4 oz ground hazelnuts	1 cup ground hazelnuts
25 g/1 oz semolina	2 tablespoons semolina flour
To decorate	*For decoration*
chopped toasted hazelnuts	chopped toasted hazelnuts

Sift the flour and salt into a bowl. Rub (cut) in the butter until the mixture resembles fine breadcrumbs. Stir in the sugar. Add the egg yolk and stir together with a knife, adding a little water if necessary. Knead lightly to make a smooth dough. Leave to rest in a cool place for 30 minutes before using.

Roll out the dough and line an 18–20 cm/7–8 inch fluted flan tin (pie pan). Spread the jam evenly over the base of the flan case (pie shell).

Cream the butter, sugar and vanilla together until light and fluffy Gradually beat in the eggs. Fold in the ground hazelnuts and semolina with a metal spoon. Spread the mixture evenly over the jam. Roll out the pastry trimmings and, using a 3.5 cm/1½ inch fluted cutter, cut out rounds. Arrange the rounds on top of the tart.

Cook in a preheated moderately hot oven (190°C/375°F, Gas Mark 5) for about 45 minutes or until golden.

Serve warm or cold, sprinkled with the chopped nuts.
Serves 6

ORANGE CUSTARD TART

METRIC/IMPERIAL	AMERICAN
Flan case	*Pie shell*
175 g/6 oz plain flour	1½ cups all-purpose flour
pinch of salt	pinch of salt
75 g/3 oz butter	6 tablespoons butter
grated rind and juice of 1 orange	grated rind and juice of 1 orange
Filling	*Filling*
2 eggs	2 eggs
40 g/1½ oz caster sugar	3 tablespoons sugar
½ teaspoon vanilla essence	½ teaspoon vanilla
300 ml/½ pint milk	1¼ cups milk
grated rind of 1 orange	grated rind of 1 orange
Topping	*Topping*
chocolate curls	chocolate curls
finely shredded orange rind	finely shredded orange rind

Sift the flour and salt into a bowl. Rub (cut) in the butter until the mixture resembles fine breadcrumbs. Stir in the orange rind. Sprinkle over about 2 tablespoons orange juice and stir together with a knife. Knead lightly to make a smooth dough.

Roll out the dough and line an 18–20 cm/7–8 inch flan tin (pie pan). Flute the edge.

Whisk the eggs with the sugar and vanilla. Place the milk and orange rind in a pan and heat gently until almost boiling. Pour on to the eggs, whisking continuously. Strain the egg custard into the flan case (pie shell). Cook in a preheated hot oven (220°C/425°F, Gas Mark 7) for 10 minutes. Reduce the oven temperature to moderate (180°C/350°F, Gas Mark 4) and continue cooking for about 20 minutes until a knife inserted into the centre comes out clean. Serve warm or chilled, decorated with the chocolate curls and orange rind.
Serves 4 to 6

APRICOT SPONGE FLAN (PIE)

METRIC/IMPERIAL	AMERICAN
Sponge flan case	*Sponge cake case*
2 eggs	2 eggs
50 g/2 oz caster sugar	¼ cup sugar
50 g/2 oz plain flour	½ cup all-purpose flour
15 g/½ oz cocoa powder	1 tablespoon unsweetened cocoa
Filling	*Filling*
100 g/4 oz cream cheese	½ cup cream cheese
50 g/2 oz caster sugar	¼ cup sugar
1–2 tablespoons cream	1–2 tablespoons cream
1 × 226 g/8 oz can apricot halves, drained	1 × ½ lb can apricot halves, drained
2 tablespoons redcurrant jelly	2 tablespoons red currant jelly
1 tablespoon lemon juice	1 tablespoon lemon juice
2 tablespoons water	2 tablespoons water
To decorate	*For decoration*
angelica	angelica
blanched almonds	blanched almonds

Place the eggs and sugar in a large heatproof bowl over a pan of hot water. Whisk until the mixture is thick and light. Sift the flour and cocoa powder together. Remove the bowl from the heat and fold the flour into the whisked mixture. Spoon into a lightly oiled and floured 20 cm/8 inch sponge flan tin (Mary Ann pan). Cook in a preheated moderately hot oven (200°C/400°F, Gas Mark 6) for about 12 minutes. Turn out carefully and leave to cool on a wire tray.

Cream the cheese, sugar and cream together. Spread evenly in the sponge cake case. Arrange the apricot halves on top, cut sides down. Put the redcurrant jelly, lemon juice and water in a small pan and stir until the jelly has dissolved. Bring to the boil and boil until the glaze hangs from the spoon for a few seconds before dropping. Spoon the glaze over the apricots. Decorate with angelica and almonds.
Serves 4 to 6

PLUM AND ALMOND FLAN (PIE)

METRIC/IMPERIAL	AMERICAN
Flan case	*Pie shell*
175 g/6 oz plain flour	1½ cups all-purpose flour
100 g/4 oz butter	½ cup butter
75 g/3 oz caster sugar	6 tablespoons sugar
3 tablespoons ground almonds	3 tablespoons ground almonds
1 egg yolk, beaten with 1 tablespoon water	1 egg yolk, beaten with 1 tablespoon water
Filling	*Filling*
450 g/1 lb plums or greengages	1 lb plums or greengages
2 eggs, beaten	2 eggs, beaten
150 ml/¼ pint double cream	⅔ cup heavy cream
100 g/4 oz caster sugar	½ cup sugar
To decorate	*For decoration*
toasted flaked almonds	toasted sliced almonds

Place the flour in a bowl and rub (cut) in the butter until the mixture resembles fine breadcrumbs. Stir in the sugar and ground almonds. Add the beaten egg yolk and stir together with a knife. Knead lightly to make a smooth dough. Leave to rest in a cool place for 30 minutes before using.

Roll out the dough and line a 25 cm/10 inch flan tin (pie pan) or china flan dish. Line with greaseproof (parchment) paper and dried beans and 'bake blind' in a preheated moderately hot oven (200°C/400°F, Gas Mark 6) for 20 minutes. Remove the paper and beans a few minutes before the end of the cooking time.

Wash, halve and stone (pit) the plums. Place in the flan case (pie shell), cut sides up. Beat together the eggs, cream and sugar and pour over the plums. Cook in a moderately hot oven (190°C/375°F, Gas Mark 5) for about 35 minutes until set. Serve warm or cold, sprinkled with the toasted flaked (sliced) almonds.
Serves 6 to 8.

Lemon Treacle Tart

LEMON TREACLE TART

METRIC/IMPERIAL

Flan case
100 g/4 oz butter or block
    margarine and lard
225 g/8 oz plain flour
pinch of salt
2 tablespoons water
milk to glaze

Filling
225 g/8 oz golden syrup
grated rind of 2 lemons
2 tablespoons lemon juice
100 g/4 oz fresh white
    breadcrumbs

AMERICAN

Pie shell
½ cup butter or margarine
    and shortening
2 cups all-purpose flour
pinch of salt
2 tablespoons water
milk to glaze

Filling
⅔ cup light corn syrup
grated rind of 2 lemons
2 tablespoons lemon juice
2 cups soft white
    breadcrumbs

Cut the fat into pieces and place in the bowl of an electric mixer. Switch on to low speed. Add the sifted flour and salt and increase the mixer speed to moderate until the fat is broken up. Mix until the mixture resembles fine breadcrumbs. Sprinkle over about 2 tablespoons water and mix for a few seconds until a dough forms.

Roll out two-thirds of the dough and line a 20 cm/8 inch flan tin (pie pan). Roll out the remaining dough to a circle the same size as the flan tin (pie pan) and cut it into six strips.

Blend the syrup, lemon rind, juice and breadcrumbs together. Spread evenly into the pastry case (pie shell). Lay the pastry strips across the filling, twisting each strip and pressing the ends on to the flan edge. Brush the strips with milk. Cook in a preheated hot oven (220°C/425°F, Gas Mark 7) for about 25 minutes. Serve warm with whipped cream.
Serves 4 to 6

BAKEWELL TART

METRIC/IMPERIAL	AMERICAN
Flan case	*Pie shell*
175 g/6 oz plain flour	1½ cups all-purpose flour
pinch of salt	pinch of salt
75 g/3 oz butter or block margarine and lard	6 tablespoons butter or margarine and shortening
2 tablespoons water	2 tablespoons water
Filling	*Filling*
3 tablespoons red jam	3 tablespoons red jam
75 g/3 oz butter	6 tablespoons butter
75 g/3 oz caster sugar	6 tablespoons sugar
1 egg, beaten	1 egg, beaten
75 g/3 oz ground almonds	¾ cup ground almonds
25 g/1 oz plain flour	¼ cup all-purpose flour
40 g/1½ oz cake crumbs	3 tablespoons cake crumbs
¼ teaspoon almond essence	¼ teaspoon almond extract
1–2 tablespoons milk	1–2 tablespoons milk
Topping	*Topping*
100 g/4 oz icing sugar	1 cup confectioners' sugar
1–2 tablespoons water	1–2 tablespoons water
1 glacé cherry	1 glacé cherry

Sift the flour and salt into a bowl. Rub (cut) in the fat until the mixture resembles fine breadcrumbs. Sprinkle over about 2 tablespoons water and stir together with a knife. Knead lightly to make a smooth dough.

Roll out the dough and line an 18–20 cm/7–8 inch flan tin (pie pan). Flute the edge. Spread the jam evenly over the pastry base (pie shell).

Cream the butter and sugar together until light and fluffy. Beat in the egg. Fold in the ground almonds, flour, cake crumbs, almond essence (extract) and milk. Spread the mixture on top of the jam. Cook in a preheated moderately hot oven (190°C/375°F, Gas Mark 5) for about 45 minutes.

Sift the icing (confectioners') sugar into a bowl. Gradually add the water so that the icing is thick enough to coat the back of a spoon. Spread the icing in a circle on the cooled tart. Press the cherry in the centre.

Serves 4 to 6

PEAR AND ORANGE SPONGE FLAN (PIE)

METRIC/IMPERIAL	AMERICAN
Sponge flan case	*Sponge cake case*
2 eggs	2 eggs
50 g/2 oz caster sugar	¼ cup sugar
50 g/2 oz plain flour	½ cup all-purpose flour
15 g/½ oz cocoa powder	1 tablespoon unsweetened cocoa
Filling	*Filling*
1 × 411 g/14½ oz can pear halves	1 × 1 lb can pear halves
1 × 311 g/11 oz can mandarin orange segments	1 × 12 oz can mandarin orange segments
1 packet orange jelly	1 package orange-flavored gelatin
150 ml/¼ pint plain yogurt	⅔ cup plain yogurt
2 teaspoons arrowroot	2 teaspoons arrowroot
To decorate	*For decoration*
whipped cream	whipped cream

Place the eggs and sugar in a heatproof bowl over a pan of hot water. Whisk until the mixture is thick and light. Sift the flour and cocoa powder together thoroughly. Remove the bowl from the heat and fold the flour into the whisked mixture using a metal spoon. Spoon into a lightly oiled and floured 20 cm/8 inch sponge flan tin (Mary Ann pan). Cook in a preheated moderately hot oven (200°C/400°F, Gas Mark 6) for about 12 minutes. Carefully turn out and leave to cool on a wire tray.

Drain the pears and mandarin oranges, reserving the syrup. Pour 150 ml/¼ pint (⅔ cup) juice into a pan, add the jelly (gelatin) and heat gently, stirring, until dissolved; leave to cool. When cooled, but not set, beat in the yogurt. When the jelly mixture starts to thicken, pour into the sponge cake case and leave to set. Arrange the pear halves, cut sides down, and the orange segments on the set jelly.

Measure about 200 ml/⅓ pint (¾ cup) of the remaining fruit syrup. Blend a little of the syrup and the arrowroot to a smooth paste in a pan. Stir in the remaining juice and cook, stirring, until the glaze is smooth and coats the back of a spoon. Lightly coat the fruit with the glaze. Pipe a line of whipped cream down each pear.

Serves 6

MACAROON TARTLETS WITH MINCEMEAT

METRIC/IMPERIAL	AMERICAN
Pastry	*Pie dough*
175 g/6 oz plain flour	1½ cups all-purpose flour
pinch of salt	pinch of salt
75 g/3 oz butter	6 tablespoons butter
25 g/1 oz caster sugar	2 tablespoons sugar
1 egg yolk	1 egg yolk
Filling	*Filling*
about 4 tablespoons mincemeat	about 4 tablespoons mincemeat
2 egg whites	2 egg whites
100 g/4 oz caster sugar	½ cup sugar
100 g/4 oz ground almonds	1 cup ground almonds
few drops almond essence	few drops almond extract
flaked almonds (optional)	slivered almonds (optional)

Sift the flour and salt into a bowl. Rub in the butter until the mixture resembles fine breadcrumbs. Stir in the sugar. Add the egg yolk and stir together with a knife, adding a little water if necessary. Knead lightly to make a smooth dough. Leave to rest in a cool place for 30 minutes before using.

Roll out the dough and use to line 12 patty tins (muffin pans). Spoon a little mincemeat into the base of each tart.

Whisk the egg whites until stiff. Gradually beat in the sugar. Fold in the ground almonds and almond essence (extract). Spoon about 1 tablespoon of this mixture into each tart. Sprinkle with almonds, if using. Cook in a preheated moderate oven (180°C/350°F, Gas Mark 4) for about 25 minutes. Leave the tartlets to cool on a wire tray.
Makes 12

Pear and Orange Sponge Flan (Pie); Bakewell Tart

DUKE OF CAMBRIDGE TART

METRIC/IMPERIAL	AMERICAN
Flan case	*Pie shell*
175 g/6 oz plain flour	1½ cups all-purpose flour
pinch of salt	pinch of salt
75 g/3 oz butter or block margarine and lard	6 tablespoons butter or margarine and shortening
2 tablespoons water	2 tablespoons water
Filling	*Filling*
75 g/3 oz glacé cherries, chopped	⅓ cup chopped glacé cherries
25 g/1 oz angelica, finely chopped	¼ cup finely chopped angelica
25 g/1 oz sultanas	¼ cup golden raisins
25 g/1 oz chopped mixed peel	¼ cup chopped candied peel
75 g/3 oz butter	6 tablespoons butter
75 g/3 oz caster sugar	6 tablespoons sugar
2 egg yolks	2 egg yolks
icing sugar	confectioners' sugar

Sift the flour and salt into a bowl. Rub in the fat until the mixture resembles fine breadcrumbs. Sprinkle over about 2 tablespoons water and stir together with a knife. Knead lightly to make a smooth dough.

Roll out the dough and line an 18–20 cm/7–8 inch fluted flan tin (pie pan), or flan ring placed on a baking sheet. Mix the cherries, angelica, sultanas (raisins) and peel together and place on the base of the flan case (pie shell).

Place the butter, sugar and egg yolks in a pan. Slowly bring to the boil, whisking continuously. Pour into the flan case (pie shell). Cook in a preheated moderately hot oven (190°C/375°F, Gas Mark 5) for about 40 minutes. Serve warm, dusted with sifted icing (confectioners') sugar.
Serves 4 to 6

BLACK CHERRY BOATS

METRIC/IMPERIAL	AMERICAN
Pastry	*Pie dough*
175 g/6 oz plain flour	1½ cups all-purpose flour
pinch of salt	pinch of salt
75 g/3 oz butter	6 tablespoons butter
25 g/1 oz caster sugar	2 tablespoons sugar
1 egg yolk	1 egg yolk
Filling	*Filling*
2 eggs	2 eggs
50 g/2 oz caster sugar	¼ cup caster sugar
25 g/1 oz plain flour	¼ cup all-purpose flour
25 g/1 oz cornflour	¼ cup cornstarch
300 ml/½ pint milk	1¼ cups milk
few drops vanilla essence	few drops vanilla
1 × 425 g/15 oz can black cherries, stoned	1 × 1 lb can bing cherries, pitted
1 teaspoon arrowroot	1 teaspoon arrowroot
To decorate	*For decoration*
whipped cream	whipped cream
grated chocolate	grated chocolate

Sift the flour and salt into a bowl. Rub in the butter until the mixture resembles fine breadcrumbs. Stir in the sugar. Add the egg yolk and stir together with a knife, adding a little water if necessary. Knead lightly to make a smooth dough. Leave to rest in a cool place for 30 minutes before using.

Roll out the dough and line 12 individual boat tins (pans). Prick the bases with a fork. Cook in a preheated moderately hot oven (200°C/400°F, Gas Mark 6) for about 15 minutes until light golden brown. Remove from the tins and leave to cool on a wire tray.

Cream the eggs and sugar together until thick and pale. Beat in the sifted flour and cornflour (cornstarch) and a little of the milk to make a paste. Place the remaining milk in a pan and, when almost boiling, pour on to the egg mixture, stirring. Return to the pan and bring the mixture to the boil, stirring; add the vanilla. Cook for 3 minutes. Remove the sauce from the heat, cover and cool.

Spread a layer of the cooled filling into each cooled pastry boat. Drain the cherries, reserving the syrup. Arrange a few of the cherries in a line down each boat. Measure 150 ml/¼ pint (⅔ cup) cherry syrup. Blend the arrowroot with a little of the syrup in a pan. Stir in the remaining juice and heat until thickened, stirring.

Glaze the fruit with the thickened cherry syrup. Pipe the cream around the edge of each boat. Sprinkle the grated chocolate over the cream.
Makes 12

CHOCOLATE BAKEWELLS

METRIC/IMPERIAL	AMERICAN
Pastry	*Pie dough*
175 g/6 oz plain flour	1½ cups all-purpose flour
pinch of salt	pinch of salt
75 g/3 oz butter or block margarine and lard	6 tablespoons butter or margarine and shortening
2 tablespoons water	2 tablespoons water
Filling	*Filling*
about 3 tablespoons raspberry or apricot jam	about 3 tablespoons raspberry or apricot jam
75 g/3 oz butter	6 tablespoons butter
75 g/3 oz caster sugar	6 tablespoons sugar
few drops almond essence	few drops almond extract
1 egg, beaten	1 egg, beaten
25 g/1 oz ground almonds	¼ cup ground almonds
50 g/2 oz self-raising flour	½ cup self-rising flour
2 tablespoons cocoa powder	2 tablespoons unsweetened cocoa
6 glacé cherries, halved	6 glacé cherries, halved

Sift the flour and salt into a bowl. Rub in the fat until the mixture resembles fine breadcrumbs. Sprinkle over about 2 tablespoons water and stir together with a knife. Knead lightly to make a smooth dough.

Roll out the dough and line 12 patty tins (muffin pans). Prick the bases with a fork. Cook in a preheated moderately hot oven (190°C/375°F, Gas Mark 5) for 10 minutes. Leave to cool and spoon a little jam into the base of each tart.

Cream the butter and sugar together until light and fluffy. Mix in the almond essence (extract) and then beat in the egg. Stir in the ground almonds. Sift the flour and cocoa together thoroughly and fold into the mixture with a metal spoon. Place a spoonful of mixture into each tartlet case. Roll out the pastry trimmings into strips, twist each strip and make a cross on each tart. Press a cherry half in the centre. Cook in a preheated moderately hot oven (190°C/375°F, Gas Mark 5) for about 25 minutes. Leave to cool on a wire tray.
Makes 12

ICED COCONUT TARTLETS

METRIC/IMPERIAL	AMERICAN
Pastry	*Pie dough*
175 g/6 oz plain flour	1½ cups all-purpose flour
pinch of salt	pinch of salt
75 g/3 oz butter	6 tablespoons butter
25 g/1 oz caster sugar	2 tablespoons sugar
1 egg yolk	1 egg yolk
Filling	*Filling*
about 3 tablespoons strawberry jam	about 3 tablespoons strawberry jam
50 g/2 oz butter	¼ cup butter
50 g/2 oz caster sugar	¼ cup sugar
1 egg, beaten	1 egg, beaten
50 g/2 oz desiccated coconut	⅔ cup shredded coconut
3 tablespoons self-raising flour	3 tablespoons self-rising flour
To decorate	*For decoration*
100 g/4 oz icing sugar	1 cup confectioners' sugar
toasted desiccated coconut	toasted shredded coconut

Sift the flour and salt into a bowl. Rub in the butter until the mixture resembles fine breadcrumbs. Stir in the sugar. Add the egg yolk and stir together with a knife, adding a little water if necessary. Knead lightly to make a smooth dough. Leave to rest in a cool place for 30 minutes before using.

Roll out the dough and line 12 to 14 patty tins (muffin pans). Spoon a little jam into the base of each case.

Cream the butter and sugar together until light and fluffy. Beat in the egg. Fold in the coconut and flour with a metal spoon. The mixture should be a soft dropping consistency; add a little milk if necessary. Place a spoonful into each tartlet case. Cook in a preheated moderately hot oven (190°C/375°F, Gas Mark 5) for about 15 minutes until golden. Turn out and leave to cool on a wire tray.

Sift the icing (confectioners') sugar into a bowl. Add about 1 tablespoon water and stir well. The icing should be thick enough to coat the back of a spoon. Spoon a little icing on to each cooled tartlet and sprinkle with a little toasted coconut.
Makes 12 to 14

PINEAPPLE MERINGUE TARTS

METRIC/IMPERIAL	AMERICAN
Pastry	*Pie dough*
175 g/6 oz plain flour	1½ cups all-purpose flour
pinch of salt	pinch of salt
75 g/3 oz butter	6 tablespoons butter
25 g/1 oz caster sugar	2 tablespoons sugar
1 egg yolk	1 egg yolk
Filling	*Filling*
1 × 376 g/13¼ oz can pineapple pieces	1 × 12 oz can pineapple pieces
25 g/1 oz butter	2 tablespoons butter
25 g/1 oz cornflour	¼ cup cornstarch
50 g/2 oz caster sugar	¼ cup sugar
2 egg yolks	2 egg yolks
Meringue	*Meringue*
2 egg whites	2 egg whites
50 g/2 oz caster sugar	¼ cup sugar

Sift the flour and salt into a bowl. Rub in the butter until the mixture resembles fine breadcrumbs. Stir in the sugar. Add the egg yolk and stir together with a knife, adding a little water if necessary. Knead lightly to make a smooth dough. Leave to rest in a cool place for 30 minutes before using.

Roll out the dough and line 12 deep patty tins (muffin pans). Prick the bases with a fork. Cook in a preheated moderately hot oven (200°C/400F, Gas Mark 6) for about 10 minutes.

Drain the pineapple, reserving the syrup and chop the pieces. Place the butter, cornflour (cornstarch), pineapple syrup made up to 300 ml/½ pint (1¼ cups) with water, and sugar in a pan. Bring to the boil, whisking, and simmer for 3 minutes. Cool slightly. Beat in the egg yolks and stir in the pineapple. Spoon into the tartlet cases.

Whisk the egg whites until stiff. Whisk in half the sugar and fold in the remainder. Spoon or pipe some meringue on to each tart. Cook in a moderately hot oven (200°C/400°F, Gas Mark 6) for about 10 minutes until the meringue is lightly browned. Serve warm.
Makes 12

Black Cherry Boats; Chocolate Bakewell; Pineapple Meringue Tart; Iced Coconut Tartlet

PARTY CHEESECAKES AND FLANS

Savoury and sweet cheesecakes for entertaining with style but without spending too much time or money.

WHOLEMEAL PIZZA FLAN (PIE)

METRIC/IMPERIAL	AMERICAN
1 × 300 g/10 oz packet brown bread mix	1 × 10 oz package brown bread mix
2 tablespoons oil	2 tablespoons oil
1 onion, chopped	1 onion, chopped
1 clove garlic, crushed	1 clove garlic, crushed
1 green pepper, cored, seeded and chopped	1 green pepper, seeded and chopped
1 teaspoon dried oregano	1 teaspoon dried oregano
100 g/4 oz button mushrooms, sliced	1 cup sliced button mushrooms
450 g/1 lb tomatoes, skinned and chopped	1 lb tomatoes, peeled and chopped
salt and pepper	salt and pepper
Topping	*Topping*
100 g/4 oz Cheddar cheese, grated	1 cup grated Cheddar cheese
25 g/1 oz Parmesan cheese	$\frac{1}{4}$ cup Parmesan cheese
25 g/1 oz wheatgerm	$\frac{1}{4}$ cup wheatgerm
25 g/1 oz sesame seeds	$\frac{1}{4}$ cup sesame seeds

Make up the bread mix, following the instructions on the pack. Roll out the dough and line a greased 28 × 18 cm/11 × 7 inch shallow oblong tin. Cover with plastic wrap and leave to rise while preparing the filling.

Heat the oil in a frying pan and fry the onion and garlic for about 5 minutes until softened. Add the green pepper and fry for a further 5 minutes. Add the oregano, mushrooms, tomatoes and salt and pepper to taste. Bring to the boil, reduce the heat and cook gently for 10 minutes.

Spread the filling over the bread base. Mix together the topping ingredients and sprinkle over the filling. Cook in a preheated moderately hot oven (200°C/400°F, Gas Mark 6) for 40 minutes. Cut into portions and serve hot or cold.

Serves 6

BLUE CHEESE AND BACON FLAN (PIE)

METRIC/IMPERIAL	AMERICAN
Flan case	*Pie shell*
100 g/4 oz plain flour	1 cup all-purpose flour
50 g/2 oz wholemeal flour	$\frac{1}{2}$ cup wholemeal flour
75 g/3 oz butter	$\frac{1}{3}$ cup butter
2 tablespoons cold water	2 tablespoons cold water
Filling	*Filling*
100 g/4 oz blue cheese, crumbled	1 cup crumbled blue cheese
175 g/6 oz cream cheese	$\frac{3}{4}$ cup cream cheese
3 eggs	3 eggs
150 ml/$\frac{1}{4}$ pint single cream	$\frac{2}{3}$ cup light cream
2 tablespoons snipped chives	2 tablespoons snipped chives
salt and pepper	salt and pepper
4 rashers streaky bacon, derinded	4 bacon slices, derinded
Garnish	*Garnish*
watercress sprigs	watercress sprigs

Place the flours in a bowl. Rub (cut) in the butter until the mixture resembles fine breadcrumbs. Add the water and mix to a firm dough. Turn out on to a lightly floured surface and knead gently. Roll out and line a 25 cm/10 inch flan tin (pie pan). Cook in a preheated hot oven (220°C/425°F, Gas Mark 7) for 10 minutes.

Cream together the two cheeses. Beat in the eggs, cream, chives and salt and pepper to taste. Pour into the flan case (pie shell) and cook in a moderately hot oven (190°C/375°F, Gas Mark 5) for 30 minutes until the filling is set.

Stretch the bacon rashers with the back of a knife; cut each in half and roll up. Grill (broil) the bacon rolls for 3 minutes until cooked. Place the rolls around the edge of flan (pie) with watercress sprigs in between. Serve warm.

Serves 8

Blue Cheese and Bacon Flan (Pie); Spanakopita

SPANAKOPITA

METRIC/IMPERIAL	AMERICAN
450 g/1 lb chopped cooked spinach	2 cups chopped cooked spinach
salt and pepper	salt and pepper
6 eggs, beaten	6 eggs, beaten
225 g/8 oz feta cheese, crumbled	2 cups feta cheese, crumbled
2 tablespoons olive oil	2 tablespoons olive oil
1 onion, finely chopped	1 onion, finely chopped
1 teaspoon dried oregano	1 teaspoon dried oregano
75 g/3 oz butter, melted	$\frac{1}{3}$ cup butter, melted
450 g/1 lb filo pastry*	1 lb filo pastry*

Mix together the spinach, salt, pepper, eggs and cheese. Heat the oil in a large pan and fry the onion for about 5 minutes until softened. Remove from the heat and add the spinach mixture and oregano, stirring well.

Generously butter a 23×33 cm (9×13 inch) baking pan. Reserve 4 sheets of filo pastry and fit the remainder into the pan, buttering each sheet as you go. The sheets will overhang the edges of pan. Pour the filling into the pan, then fold over ends of pastry sheets to cover it. Butter remaining sheets of pastry and fold over to size of dish. Place on top of dish and brush with butter. Make three slits in pastry with a sharp knife. Cook in a preheated moderately hot oven (190°C/375°F, Gas Mark 5) for 45 to 50 minutes until the pastry is crisp and golden brown. Cut into squares to serve.

Serves 8

*Note: filo pastry can be bought from Greek food shops and delicatessens.

FROSTED GRAPE CHEESECAKE

METRIC/IMPERIAL	AMERICAN
Base	*Base*
50 g/2 oz butter, melted	¼ cup butter, melted
75 g/3 oz crushed cornflakes	3 cups crushed cornflakes
25 g/1 oz sugar	2 tablespoons sugar
Filling	*Filling*
15 g/½ oz gelatine	2 envelopes unflavored
3 tablespoons water	gelatin
350 g/12 oz curd cheese	3 tablespoons water
grated rind and juice of 1	1½ cups curd cheese
orange	grated rind and juice of 1
100 g/4 oz caster sugar	orange
2 egg whites	½ cup sugar
Topping	2 egg whites
225 g/8 oz black grapes	*Topping*
1 egg white	½ lb purple grapes
caster sugar	1 egg white
150 ml/¼ pint soured cream	sugar
	⅔ cup sour cream

Mix together the butter, cornflakes and sugar and press over
the bottom of an 18 cm/7 inch loose-bottomed cake tin
(springform pan). Chill the base while preparing the filling.

Put the gelatine and water into a small heatproof bowl over a
pan of hot water and stir until the gelatine has dissolved.
Leave to cool slightly. Mix together the cheese, orange rind
and juice and sugar. Stir in the gelatine. Whisk the egg whites
until stiff and fold into the cheese mixture. Pour on to the
cornflake base and chill for about 2 hours until set.

Wash the grapes and dry well. Divide into bunches of two
or three grapes and brush with egg white. Toss in sugar and
leave to dry. Remove the cheesecake from the pan and
spread the top with soured cream. Arrange the bunches of
frosted grapes on the cheesecake and serving plate.
Serves 6

VOL-AU-VENT TOULOUSE

METRIC/IMPERIAL	AMERICAN
200 g/7 oz frozen puff pastry,	7 oz frozen puff pastry,
thawed	thawed
beaten egg to glaze	beaten egg to glaze
1 large chicken breast	1 large chicken breast
portion	portion
1 carrot, chopped	1 carrot, chopped
1 onion, chopped	1 onion, chopped
1 bouquet garni	1 bouquet garni
40 g/1½ butter	3 tablespoons butter
40 g/1½ oz plain flour	6 tablespoons all-purpose
100 g/4 oz cooked ham,	flour
chopped	½ cup chopped cooked ham
100 g/4 oz mushrooms,	1 cup chopped mushrooms
chopped	salt and pepper
salt and pepper	1 egg yolk
1 egg yolk	2 tablespoons light cream
2 tablespoons single cream	

Roll out the pastry and cut out a 20 cm/8 inch round. Place on a
damp baking sheet. With the point of a sharp knife, cut a circle
halfway through the thickness of pastry and 2.5 cm/1 inch from
the edge. Brush with beaten egg and mark lightly in a criss-
cross pattern. Cook in a preheated hot oven (220°C/425°F,
Gas Mark 7) for 25 minutes until well risen and golden.
Carefully remove the pastry lid and scoop out the soft centre.
Return to the oven for 5 minutes.

Meanwhile place the chicken, carrot, onion and bouquet
garni in a saucepan with water to cover and bring to the boil.
Reduce the heat, cover and simmer for 30 minutes until the
chicken is tender. Strain off the stock and reserve 300 ml/½ pint
(1¼ cups). Remove any bones from the chicken and chop the
meat.

Melt the butter in a pan, add the flour and cook for 1 minute.
Gradually stir in the reserved stock and cook until the sauce is
smooth and thickened. Add the ham, chicken, mushrooms
and salt and pepper to taste and cook for a further 5 minutes.
Beat together the egg yolk and cream. Remove the sauce from
the heat and beat in the egg and cream mixture. Spoon the
sauce into the vol-au-vent case and top with the lid. Serve hot.
Serves 4

MIXED FRUIT JALOUSIE

METRIC/IMPERIAL	AMERICAN
200 g/7 oz frozen puff pastry, thawed	7 oz frozen puff pastry, thawed
beaten egg to glaze	beaten egg for glaze
450 g/1 lb fruit (e.g. grapes, peach slices, raspberries, strawberries)	1 lb fruit (e.g. grapes, peach slices, raspberries, strawberries)
2 tablespoons apricot jam	2 tablespoons apricot jam
2 tablespoons sugar	2 tablespoons sugar
2 tablespoons water	2 tablespoons water

Roll out the pastry to an oblong 25 × 15 cm (10 × 6 inches). Fold it over lengthwise and cut out a rectangle from folded edge, leaving a 2.5 cm (1 inch) wide border round edge. Unfold the pastry. Roll out centre rectangle to the same size as pastry border. Place pastry base on a damp baking sheet and brush with egg. Lay pastry border carefully on top and press to seal. Flute the edges. Brush pastry border with egg and prick the base. Cook in a preheated hot oven (220°C/425°F, Gas Mark 7) for 20 to 25 minutes until risen and golden. Leave to cool on a wire rack.

Arrange the fruits in rows in the base of jalousie. Place jam, sugar and water in a small saucepan. Heat gently to dissolve sugar, then boil for 2 minutes. Press through a sieve, then brush over the fruits.
Serves 6

Mixed Fruit Jalousie; Vol-au-Vent Toulouse

CARIBBEAN CHEESECAKE

METRIC/IMPERIAL	AMERICAN
Base	*Base*
2 tablespoons golden syrup	2 tablespoons light corn syrup
50 g/2 oz margarine	$\frac{1}{4}$ cup margarine
225 g/8 oz gingernut biscuits, crushed	$\frac{1}{2}$ lb gingersnap cookies, crushed
Filling	*Filling*
225 g/8 oz cottage cheese, sieved	1 cup cottage cheese, sieved
grated rind and juice of 1 lemon	grated rind and juice of 1 lemon
2 tablespoons dark rum	2 tablespoons dark rum
25 g/1 oz butter, melted	2 tablespoons butter, melted
50 g/2 oz caster sugar	$\frac{1}{4}$ cup sugar
1 egg, beaten	1 egg, beaten
4 small ripe bananas	4 small ripe bananas
Topping	*Topping*
2 teaspoons arrowroot	2 teaspoons arrowroot
25 g/1 oz caster sugar	2 tablespoons sugar

Place the syrup and margarine in a pan and heat together until melted. Stir in the biscuit (cookie) crumbs. Press the crumb mixture over the bottom and up the sides of a 20 cm/8 inch flan tin (pie pan).

Mix together the cheese, lemon rind, rum, melted butter, sugar and egg. Slice two bananas and place on the crumb base. Pour the cheesecake mixture over the bananas and smooth the top. Cook in a preheated moderate oven (160°C/325°F, Gas Mark 3) for 20 minutes until the filling has just set. Leave to cool.

Make the lemon juice up to 150 ml/$\frac{1}{4}$ pint ($\frac{2}{3}$ cup) with water. Blend the arrowroot with a little of the liquid. Place the arrowroot and remaining lemon juice mixture in a pan with the sugar. Bring to the boil, stirring, and cook until thickened and smooth. Leave to cool. Slice the remaining bananas and arrange over the cheesecake. Spoon over glaze and chill.
Serves 4 to 6

CHANTILLY GINGER CHEESECAKE

METRIC/IMPERIAL
Base 100 g/4 oz plain flour
50 g/2 oz butter
25 g/1 oz caster sugar
1 egg, beaten
Filling
400 g/14 oz full fat soft cheese
100 g/4 oz sugar
2 eggs
2 teaspoons lemon juice
1 tablespoon freshly grated
   root ginger
Topping
150 ml/¼ pint double cream
crystallized ginger

AMERICAN
Base
1 cup all-purpose flour
¼ cup butter
2 tablespoons sugar
1 egg, beaten
Filling
2 × ½ lb package
   cream cheese
½ cup sugar
2 eggs
2 teaspoons lemon juice
1 tablespoon freshly grated
   ginger root
Topping
⅔ cup heavy cream
crystallized ginger

Sift the flour into a bowl. Add the butter, cut into small pieces, and rub (cut) in until the mixture resembles fine breadcrumbs. Stir in the sugar. Add the egg and mix to a firm dough. Turn out on to a lightly floured surface and knead gently. Roll out and line a buttered 23 cm/9 inch pie dish (pie shell). Crimp the edges to decorate. Line with greaseproof (parchment) paper and dried beans and 'bake blind' in a preheated moderately hot oven (200°C/400°F, Gas Mark 6) for 10 minutes. Remove the paper and beans.

Beat the cheese until softened. Beat in the sugar, eggs, lemon juice and root ginger. Pour into the pastry case (pie shell) and cook in a moderate oven (180°C/350°F, Gas Mark 4) for 25 minutes, until the filling has set. Leave to cool.

Whip the cream until thick. Spread over the cheesecake and decorate with slices of crystallized ginger.
Serves 6

Apple and Almond Meringue Flan (Pie); Chantilly Ginger Cheesecake

APPLE AND ALMOND MERINGUE FLAN (PIE)

METRIC/IMPERIAL	AMERICAN
Flan case	*Pie shell*
175 g/6 oz plain flour	1½ cups all-purpose flour
100 g/4 oz butter	½ cup butter
25 g/1 oz caster sugar	2 tablespoons sugar
1 egg yolk	1 egg yolk
a little water	a little water
Filling	*Filling*
300 ml/½ pint apple purée	1¼ cups applesauce
25 g/1 oz sugar	2 tablespoons sugar
grated rind and juice of ½ lemon	grated rind and juice of ½ lemon
2 egg yolks	2 egg yolks
75 g/3 oz ground almonds	¾ cup ground almonds
Meringue	*Meringue*
2 egg whites	2 egg whites
100 g/4 oz caster sugar	½ cup sugar

Sift the flour into a bowl. Add the butter, cut into small pieces, and rub (cut) in until the mixture resembles fine breadcrumbs. Stir in the sugar. Add the egg yolk and just enough water to make a firm dough. Turn out on to a floured surface and knead lightly. Roll out and line a 20 cm/8 inch flan tin (pie pan). Prick the base and cook in a preheated moderately hot oven (200°C/400°F, Gas Mark 6) for 15 minutes.

Mix together the apple, sugar, lemon rind and juice, egg yolks and ground almonds. Spread in the pastry case (pie shell). Whisk the egg whites until stiff and dry. Whisk in 1 tablespoon sugar, then carefully fold in remaining sugar. Spoon the meringue into a large piping (pastry) bag with a large star nozzle attached. Pipe the meringue over the flan to completely cover the filling. Cook in a preheated moderate oven (180°C/350°F, Gas Mark 4) for 25 minutes until the meringue is crisp and golden. Serve warm.
Serves 4 to 6

MARBLED CHOCOLATE CHEESECAKE

METRIC/IMPERIAL	AMERICAN
Filling	*Filling*
100 g/4 oz caster sugar	½ cup sugar
3 eggs, separated	3 eggs, separated
150 ml/¼ pint milk	⅔ cup milk
450 g/1 lb cream cheese	2 cups cream cheese
15 g/½ oz gelatine	2 envelopes gelatin
3 tablespoons water	3 tablespoons water
75 g/3 oz plain chocolate	3 squares (1 oz each) semi-sweet chocolate
150 ml/¼ pint double cream	⅔ cup heavy cream
few drops of vanilla essence	few drops of vanilla
Base	*Base*
100 g/4 oz digestive biscuits, crushed	1 cup crushed graham crackers
50 g/2 oz caster sugar	¼ cup sugar
50 g/2 oz butter, melted	¼ cup butter, melted

Place the sugar and egg yolks in a heatproof bowl and beat until light and frothy. Heat the milk in a pan and pour into the bowl, stirring. Place the bowl over a pan of boiling water and cook the egg mixture, stirring, until thickened and smooth. Remove the bowl from the heat and set aside until completely cold.

Beat the cream cheese until smooth, then beat in the egg custard. Put the gelatine and water into a small heatproof bowl over a pan of hot water and stir until the gelatine has dissolved. Leave to cool slightly, then fold into the cheese mixture. Melt the chocolate in a bowl over hot water and cool slightly. Whip the cream and fold into the cheese mixture.

Mix together the biscuit (cracker) crumbs, sugar and butter. Press over the base of a greased 25 cm/10 inch loose-bottomed cake tin (springform pan).

When the filling is beginning to set, place half in a separate bowl and carefully fold in the melted chocolate. Stir a few drops of vanilla into the plain mixture. Whisk the egg whites until stiff and fold half into each mixture. Place alternate spoonfuls of chocolate and vanilla mixture over the prepared base. Swirl the mixtures with a fine skewer. Leave the cheesecake in the refrigerator to set.
Serves 8

PEAR AND WALNUT FLAN (PIE)

METRIC/IMPERIAL	AMERICAN
175 g/6 oz plain flour	1½ cups all-purpose flour
1 teaspoon ground ginger	1 teaspoon ground ginger
100 g/4 oz butter	½ cup butter
50 g/2 oz caster sugar	¼ cup sugar
1 egg, beaten	1 egg, beaten
50 g/2 oz walnuts, finely chopped	½ cup finely chopped walnuts
3 ripe pears	3 ripe pears
milk and sugar, to glaze	milk and sugar for glaze
To decorate	*For decoration*
150 ml/¼ pint double cream	⅔ cup heavy cream

Sift the flour and ginger into a bowl. Add the butter, cut into small pieces, and rub (cut) in until the mixture resembles fine breadcrumbs. Add half the sugar, the egg and walnuts and mix to a firm dough. Turn out on to a floured surface and knead lightly. Roll out two-thirds of the dough and line a 20 cm/8 inch flan tin (pie pan). Peel, halve and core the pears. Arrange the pears in the pastry case (pie shell) and sprinkle with the remaining sugar. Roll out remaining pastry and cover the flan (pie). With the point of a sharp knife, cut out a 7.5 cm/3 inch circle from the centre of the dough and remove. Brush pastry with milk and sprinkle with sugar. Cook in a preheated moderately hot oven (200°C/400°F, Gas Mark 6) for about 30 minutes until golden brown. Leave until cold. Whip the cream until stiff and pipe in centre of flan (pie).
Serves 4 to 6

DANISH CHRISTMAS CHEESECAKE

METRIC/IMPERIAL	AMERICAN
150 g/5 oz butter	¾ cup butter
200 g/7 oz caster sugar	1 cup sugar
175 g/6 oz carrots, grated	1 cup grated carrots
½ teaspoon salt	½ teaspoon salt
1 teaspoon ground cinnamon	1 teaspoon ground cinnamon
2 eggs	2 eggs
200 g/7 oz self-raising flour	2 cups self-rising flour
100 g/4 oz raisins	¾ cup raisins
Frosting	*Frosting*
50 g/2 oz softened butter	¼ cup softened butter
100 g/4 oz full fat soft cheese	1 × ¼ lb package cheese
100 g/4 oz sifted icing sugar	1 cup sifted confectioners' sugar
½ teaspoon vanilla essence	½ teaspoon vanilla

Gently melt the butter and pour into a mixing bowl. Beat in the sugar, grated carrot, salt, cinnamon and eggs. Fold in the flour and raisins. Pour into a buttered 18 cm/7 inch square cake tin (baking pan). Cook in a preheated moderate oven (160°C/325°F, Gas Mark 3) for about 45 minutes until golden brown and firm to the touch. Leave to cool in the tin for 5 minutes, then turn out on to a wire rack to cool completely.

Beat together the softened butter and cheese until smooth, then gradually beat in the sugar and vanilla. Spread the frosting evenly over top and sides of cake, swirling with a fork.
Serves 6

LEMON AND LIME CHEESECAKE GATEAU

METRIC/IMPERIAL	AMERICAN
225 g/8 oz full fat soft cheese	1 × ½ lb package cream cheese
1 × 350 g/12 oz can condensed milk	1 can (¾ lb) condensed milk
120 ml/4 fl oz lemon juice	½ cup lemon juice
8 individual trifle sponge cakes	8 individual dessert sponge shells
100 g/4 oz shelled pistachio nuts	1 cup shelled pistachio nuts
150 ml/¼ pint double cream	⅔ cup heavy cream
1 lime	1 lime

Line a deep 20 cm/8 inch round cake tin (baking pan) with foil, allowing 5 cm/2 inches to stand above the rim. Place the soft cheese in a bowl and beat with a wooden spoon until smooth. Gradually beat in the condensed milk. Add the lemon juice and beat until thick. Leave to set in a cool place.

Split each sponge cake in half horizontally. Arrange a layer over the base and around inside of tin, cutting to fit. Spread one-third of the filling over the sponge base and cover with another layer of sponge. Repeat with another third of the filling and remaining sponge slices. Fold over the foil and chill for at least 3 hours.

Place the pistachio nuts in a pan with boiling water to cover. Boil for 1 minute, then drain and slip off the skins. Chop the nuts.

Fold back the foil from the cheesecake and invert on to a serving plate. Peel off the foil. Cover with the remaining filling and coat the side with chopped nuts. Whip the cream until stiff and pipe rosettes of cream around the edge of cake and in centre. Thinly slice the lime, then cut each slice into quarters. Place around cake between rosettes of cream.
Serves 6 to 8

PEACHY CHEESECAKE TARTS

METRIC/IMPERIAL	AMERICAN
Pastry	*Pie dough*
175 g/6 oz plain flour	1½ cups all-purpose flour
1 teaspoon ground cinnamon	1 teaspoon ground cinnamon
100 g/4 oz butter	½ cup butter
2 tablespoons cold water	2 tablespoons cold water
Filling	*Filling*
1 orange	1 orange
175 g/6 oz curd cheese	¾ cup curd cheese
50 g/2 oz caster sugar	¼ cup sugar
2 eggs, beaten	2 eggs, beaten
3 ripe peaches	3 ripe peaches
3 tablespoons redcurrant jelly	3 tablespoons redcurrant jelly

Sift the flour and cinnamon into a bowl. Add the butter, cut into small pieces, and rub (cut) in until the mixture resembles fine breadcrumbs. Add the water and mix to a firm dough. Knead lightly then roll out and cut out 12 rounds, using a 10 cm/4 inch fluted cutter. Line 12 tartlet tins with the pastry rounds. Cook in a preheated moderately hot oven (200°C/400°F, Gas Mark 6) for 10 minutes.

Finely grate the orange rind and mix with the cheese, sugar and eggs. Beat well until smooth. Pour the mixture into the pastry cases and cook in a moderately hot oven (200°C/400°F, Gas Mark 6) for 20 minutes until the filling has set. Leave to cool on a wire rack.

Slice the peaches thinly and arrange overlapping segments in the tartlets. Heat the redcurrant jelly and brush over the peaches to glaze. Serve these tartlets on the day they are made.

Makes 12

Lemon and Lime Cheesecake Gateau

INDEX

Photography by Robert Golden
Photographic stylist Antonia Gaunt
Food prepared by Mary Cadogan, assisted by Clare Gordon-Smith